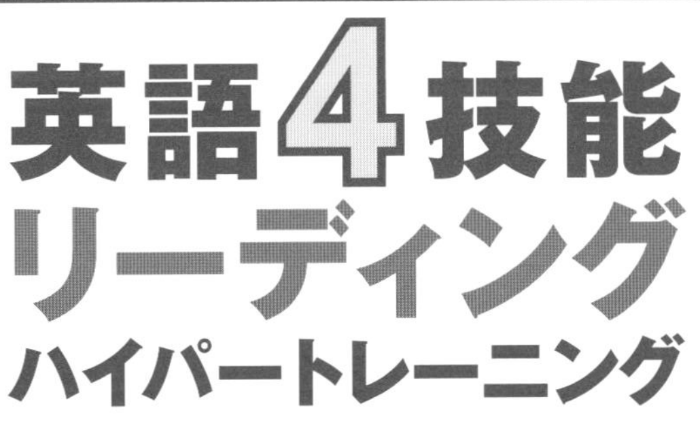

長文読解 

 基礎編

問題編

K 桐原書店

英語4技能
リーディング
ハイパートレーニング

長文読解  基礎編

問題編

Contents

桐原書店

リーディング問題に取り組むにあたって

1. パッセージ全体のテーマをとらえよう

タイトルがある文章の場合は，まず最初にタイトルを読み，何について書かれた文章なのかをつかみましょう。次に（タイトルがない文章の場合は最初に）設問に目を通します。それによって，本文のどこに注目して読むべきかがわかります。また，設問はたいてい本文の内容の順に並んでいるので，あらかじめ設問に目を通しておくことは，文章の流れを理解する手助けにもなるでしょう。選択肢まで先に細かく読む必要はありません。タイトルと設問をしっかりと読んで，どのような情報を求めてその文章を読むのかを先に知っておくようにしましょう。

2. 設問に関連する部分を探しながら読もう

試験には時間制限があるので，一文一文を細かくていねいに読んで，設問に関係しないところの文法や構文で考えこんでしまっては，時間オーバーになってしまいます。1. の作業で，本文で注目すべき場所は見当がつくはずなので，時間配分を考えながら読んでいきましょう。

3. 論理マーカーで流れをつかもう

論理マーカーとは，文と文との論理的関係を示す目印となることばです。たとえば，because（なぜなら）があれば，その前に「結果」が，その後ろに「原因」にあたることが述べられていると予想できます。また，but（しかし）なら「逆接」ですが，単にその前後が反対の内容になっているというより，「一般論」but「筆者の主張」という順番で，後ろの方に大切なことが述べられているケースもあります。また，for example（たとえば）の後には，その前に述べられていたことの具体例が続きます。このような論理マーカーを知っておくと，どこに何が書いてあるのかをつかみやすくなります。

Unit 1

⇒本冊 p.10 ～ 15

DATA
●ワード数：97 words
●目標解答時間：5分

Read the passage and choose the best answer from among the four choices for each question. Then, on your answer sheet, find the number of the question and mark your answer.

（次の英文の内容に関して，それぞれの質問に対する答えとして最も適切なものを4つの選択肢の中から一つ選び，その番号のマーク欄をぬりつぶしなさい。）

Volunteers Wanted at Ferndale Library!

We need people who love reading and spending time with children. There are many ways to help at the library:

Reading club—Children from 5 to 13 years old come to the library to practice reading. We need volunteers to help them. (Saturdays and Sundays from 1:00 p.m. to 4:00 p.m.)

Book readers—We have story time on Saturday mornings. Read a book to children under 6 years old. (Saturdays from 10:30 a.m. to 11:30 a.m.)

Computer teachers—Teach kids to use computers. (Mondays and Wednesdays from 5:00 p.m. to 6:00 p.m.)

(1) What is this notice for?

1 To find people to help at the library.
2 To sell books to children.
3 To tell people about a new library.
4 To find people to babysit children.

(1) ① ② ③ ④

(2) When can people help children with their reading practice?

1 On weekends between 1:00 p.m. and 4:00 p.m.
2 On Saturdays between 10:30 a.m. and 11:30 a.m.
3 On Sundays between 10:30 a.m. and 11:30 a.m.
4 On weekdays between 5:00 p.m. and 6:00 p.m.

(2) ① ② ③ ④

Unit 2

⇒本冊 p.16 ~ 21

DATA
●ワード数：92 words
●目標解答時間：5分

Read the passage and choose the best answer from among the four choices for each question. Then, on your answer sheet, find the number of the question and mark your answer.

Collingwood Park

Have fun seeing the beautiful plants in Collingwood Park. Our guide, Richard Wilson, teaches you many interesting things about the trees and flowers. This month, the lavenders are beautiful. If you're lucky, you may also see a deer! Bring your camera.

Our walks start every Sunday at 10:00 a.m. We leave from the east baseball field. The walk ends at the visitor center at 11:30 a.m. To get to the park, take the Green Line to Collingwood Station or Bus #17 to the Glenwood Town.

Call 555-4267 for more information.

(1) What can people do with Richard Wilson on Sundays at 10:00 a.m.?

1 Plant flowers.
2 Play baseball.
3 Learn about nature.
4 Clean up the park.

(2) Where will the people meet?

1 Collingwood Station.
2 Glenwood Town.
3 The visitor center.
4 The east baseball field.

 ⇒本冊 p.22 ～ 27

DATA
●ワード数：100 words
●目標解答時間：5 分

Read the passage and choose the best answer from among the four choices for each question. Then, on your answer sheet, find the number of the question and mark your answer.

Do you like robots?

We can teach you how to make a robot yourself. After you make it, you can play with your robot! You can make robots for racing, picking things up, and climbing.

Class A: Beginner class (Monday and Wednesday from 5:00 p.m. to 6:00 p.m., June 4 – July 25. Cost: $250)
Class B: Advanced class (Tuesday and Friday from 5:00 p.m. to 6:30 p.m., June 5 – July 27. Cost: $300)

On Saturday, June 2 at 10:00 a.m., you can take a special class to try making robots. It's free!

Supertech Robot School
23 Windemere Lane
Telephone: 555-2452

(1) This notice is for people who want to
1 watch a robot-building contest.
2 make their own robots.
3 watch a robot race.
4 buy a toy robot.

(2) When can people take a free class?
1 On June 2.
2 On June 4.
3 On June 5.
4 On July 25.

(2) ① ② ③ ④

Unit 4

⇒本冊 p.28 ~ 33

DATA
●ワード数：105 words
●目標解答時間：5 分

Read the passage and choose the best answer from among the four choices for each question. Then, on your answer sheet, find the number of the question and mark your answer.

To All Students

The famous writer Todd Burnett is coming to Northview High School. He has visited 30 different countries, and he writes about the places he visited in his books. He is going to talk about some of the interesting places that he has visited. He will also show 50 photos of his favorite places. Mr. Burnett has written more than 20 books, and many of them are bestsellers.

Where: The school library
When: September 21 at 3:30 p.m.

You can sign up* by writing your name on the whiteboard outside the school office. There will be only 40 seats, so sign up quickly!

*sign up: 申し込む

(1) What will happen on September 21?

1 A writer will talk about different countries.
2 Students from another country will visit.
3 There will be a book sale.
4 Class photos will be taken.

(2) How many people can go to the event?

1 20.
2 30.
3 40.
4 50.

(2) ① ② ③ ④

⇒本冊 p.34 ~ 39

DATA
●ワード数：122 words
●目標解答時間：5 分

Read the passage and choose the best answer from among the four choices for each question. Then, on your answer sheet, find the number of the question and mark your answer.

Show Us Your Talent*!

Redford Senior High School is inviting people who can take part in this year's talent show on November 12.
If you can sing, play music, dance, or do magic, you can be in the show. Your performance must be between 2 and 8 minutes long. We need 15 performers for the show.
First prize will be a free dinner at Rocky's Hamburgers. Second prize will be a $30 gift coupon from Pressler Books. Third prize will be a T-shirt from Collier Fashions.
We also need 8 volunteers to sell tickets and clean up after the show.
If you would like to be in the talent show, sign up in Ms. Cameron's homeroom by 4:00 p.m. on October 30.

*talent: 才能

(1) How many people will be in the talent show?

1 Two.
2 Eight.
3 Twelve.
4 Fifteen.

(1)	① ② ③ ④

(2) The best performer will get

1 a gift coupon.
2 a T-shirt.
3 free food.
4 a dance lesson.

(2)	① ② ③ ④

Unit 6

⇒本冊 p.40 ~ 49

DATA
●ワード数：253 words
●目標解答時間：10 分

Read the passage and choose the best answer from among the four choices for each question. Then, on your answer sheet, find the number of the question and mark your answer.

From: Bradley Hawkins
To: Jane Wilson
Date: August 28
Subject: Thanks!

Hi Aunt Jane,
Thanks so much for letting me stay at your house again this summer. It's really beautiful at Lake Deerfield, and it was fun to go swimming with you and Uncle Martin every morning. After we got home, Mom took me to the pool, and she was surprised because I can swim twice as far now. I'll never forget driving the motorboat. No one ever let me do that before. I enjoyed going really fast all around the lake. It was exciting. Please tell Uncle Martin again that I'm sorry about his fishing pole. I was not careful with it. Mom says, "Thank you for the jam." It was fun picking strawberries and blueberries. You make the best jam I've ever eaten! I hope I can stay with you again next year.
Love,
Bradley

From: Jane Wilson
To: Bradley Hawkins
Date: August 29
Subject: Thanks for coming

Hi Bradley,
We're glad you had a good time with us. Don't worry about the fishing pole. Everybody drops things sometimes. Uncle Martin fixed it yesterday, and it works fine now. He caught three fish this morning. We took lots of pictures of you at the cottage, so we're going to send them to you soon. I think you'll like the picture of you and the hamburgers. We were surprised that you could eat five of them. We

hope that you'll be able to stay with us again next summer.
Love,
Aunt Jane

(1) What did Bradley do for the first time?

1 He stayed at his aunt's house.
2 He drove a motorboat.
3 He learned to swim.
4 He went fishing.

(2) What did Aunt Jane give to Bradley's mother?

1 Some jam.
2 Some photos.
3 Some fish.
4 Some hamburgers.

(3) Why is Bradley sorry?

1 He broke his uncle's fishing pole.
2 He stayed too long at the cottage.
3 He broke the motorboat.
4 He ate too much jam.

Unit 7

⇒本冊 p.50 ~ 61

DATA
●ワード数：286 words
●目標解答時間：10 分

Read the passage and choose the best answer from among the four choices for each question. Then, on your answer sheet, find the number of the question and mark your answer.

From: Wendy Pierce
To: Barbara Pierce
Date: September 22
Subject: Thank you

Dear Grandma,
Thank you very much for the birthday money. I was planning to buy a new soccer ball or a watch, but I saw a video game, and I bought that. It's really fun, but Mom says I can only play it for 30 minutes every day. I'm busy because I have to practice the clarinet for our school concert. We practice for one hour in the morning. Then after school, we have another practice for 90 minutes. Can you come to the concert? It will be on Saturday, October 2. It will start at 2:00 p.m., and it will be about two hours long.
Love,
Wendy

From: Barbara Pierce
To: Wendy Pierce
Date: September 25
Subject: Concert

Dear Wendy,
I'm happy to hear you're enjoying the video game. It's great that you're practicing the clarinet so much. I want to go to your concert, but I will travel to Weston that weekend. I'm going to visit a friend of mine who lives there. I already bought tickets, so I can't change my plans. I know that you're a great clarinet player, so I'm sure the concert will be very good.
Love,
Grandma

From: Wendy Pierce
To: Barbara Pierce
Date: October 2
Subject: All done!

Dear Grandma,

I played in the concert today! I was nervous*, but everybody clapped* a lot for our performance. Thank you for sending the flowers. I was really surprised to get them. Also, Mom borrowed a video camera from her friend. She took a video, so you will be able to see it all. She'll send it to you soon. I hope you will enjoy it.

Love,

Wendy

*nervous: 神経質な

*clap: 拍手する

(1) What did Wendy buy with the money from Grandma?

1 A soccer ball.

2 A watch.

3 A video game.

4 A clarinet.

(1)	① ② ③ ④

(2) How long does Wendy practice after school?

1 Thirty minutes.

2 One hour.

3 Ninety minutes.

4 Two hours.

(2)	① ② ③ ④

(3) What did Wendy's mother do?

1 She made a video of the concert.

2 She gave flowers to Wendy.

3 She bought tickets for Wendy's grandmother.

4 She invited her friend to the concert.

(3)	① ② ③ ④

Unit 8

⇒本冊 p.62 ~ 71

DATA
●ワード数：286 words
●目標解答時間：10 分

Read the passage and choose the best answer from among the four choices for each question. Then, on your answer sheet, find the number of the question and mark your answer.

From: Teresa Pearson
To: Sophie LaRue
Date: May 9
Subject: Request

Dear Ms. LaRue,
I am a writer for the Pennington High School newspaper, and I am working on* an article about you and your clothes. I read in a magazine that you won the Young Fashion Designer of the Year award this year, and I thought your clothes were beautiful. I know that you are very busy, but I would really like to ask you some questions about your work. I would like to talk to you for about 10 minutes on the phone.
Yours Truly,
Teresa Pearson

*work on: 取り組む

From: Sophie LaRue
To: Teresa Pearson
Date: May 10
Subject: Your request

Dear Teresa,
Thank you for your e-mail. I was happy to hear that you read about me in the magazine. I'm very busy right now because I will have a fashion show on May 27. Two days after the fashion show, I am going on a trip to Paris. I am free only on May 28. I will have meetings in the morning, but you could call me in the afternoon. My phone number is 555-2985.
Sincerely,
Sophie LaRue

From: Teresa Pearson
To: Sophie LaRue
Date: May 29
Subject: Thank you

Dear Ms. LaRue,
Thank you so much for talking to me yesterday! And thank you also for the drawings you gave me. We're going to put them in the newspaper next to the article. I think the article is going to be really interesting. I will finish writing it this weekend. The next issue* of the school newspaper will be published* on Wednesday next week. I'll send you a copy then!
Yours Truly,
Teresa Pearson

*the next issue: 次号
*publish: 発行する

(1) Teresa wants to ask Ms. LaRue about
1 starting a fashion magazine.
2 working in her clothing store.
3 her job of a fashion designer.
4 who will win the design award.

(2) What will Sophie LaRue do on May 29?
1 Write an article for a fashion magazine.
2 Have a fashion show.
3 Go to a meeting.
4 Travel to Paris.

(3) What will Teresa do next week?
1 Send a copy of her article to Sophie LaRue.
2 Call Sophie LaRue again.
3 Give Sophie LaRue her drawings.
4 Finish writing the article about Sophie LaRue.

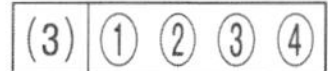

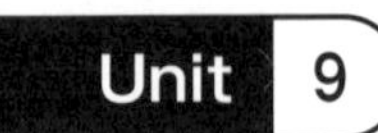

⇒本冊 p.72 ~ 83

DATA
●ワード数：274 words
●目標解答時間：10 分

Read the passage and choose the best answer from among the four choices for each question. Then, on your answer sheet, find the number of the question and mark your answer.

From: Laura Higgins
To: Marla Brantford
Date: January 14
Subject: Green Mountain Ski Resort

Hi Marla,
How are you? My parents and I are going to Green Mountain Ski Resort next month. If you're free, would you like to come with us? We can go on February 7 or 14. Green Mountain is a great resort, but it's a long way from my house. We're going to leave at around 5:00 a.m. and drive until 8:00 a.m. We'll ski all day from 9:00 a.m. and then leave the resort at around 5:00 p.m. We'll get home at around 10:00 p.m. Please tell me if you can come.
Your friend,
Laura

From: Marla Brantford
To: Laura Higgins
Date: January 15
Subject: I can go!

Hi Laura,
Thanks for asking me. I can go on February 14, but I have to visit my grandma's house on the other day. I don't have any skis, but my older brother said I could use his. I also want to buy a new ski jacket. I want to look good while I'm skiing! Do you want to come shopping with me this weekend?
Your friend,
Marla

From: Laura Higgins
To: Marla Brantford
Date: January 15
Subject: Shopping

Hi Marla,
I'm glad you can come with us! And yes, I want to go to the mall with you. I got $60 for my birthday, so I want to buy a warm sweater. Mom says she can pay for your lift ticket and food at the ski resort. Last time, you had a nice camera, and you took photos with it. Could you bring it again this time?
Your friend,
Laura

(1) Laura says that Green Mountain Ski Resort
1 has free skiing in February.
2 is her favorite place to ski.
3 is far from her house.
4 opens at 8 a.m.

(1) ① ② ③ ④

(2) Marla can't go skiing on February 7 because
1 she has to see her grandma.
2 she has to go shopping.
3 her brother needs his skis.
4 the ski resort will be closed.

(3) Laura asks Marla to bring
1 a warm sweater.
2 some money.
3 some food.
4 a camera.

(3) ① ② ③ ④

Unit 10

⇒本冊 p.84 ~ 95

DATA
●ワード数：281 words
●目標解答時間：10 分

Read the passage and choose the best answer from among the four choices for each question. Then, on your answer sheet, find the number of the question and mark your answer.

From: Melanie Jones
To: Dan Campbell
Date: October 1
Subject: Your poster

Dear Dan,
I saw your poster at Super Sounds Music Store last Sunday. It says that your band needs a new guitar player. I started playing the guitar five years ago. I was in a band during high school, but I moved to Springfield at the beginning of last month. Now I'm a college student, and I want to find a new band and play with new members. I usually play rock and pop music. I'd like to join you.
Melanie

From: Dan Campbell
To: Melanie Jones
Date: October 1
Subject: Hello

Dear Melanie,
Thanks for your e-mail. All the members of our band go to Springfield University. Is that the university you go to? I got e-mails from three people who want to be in our band, so we're inviting everyone and will listen to you all play for us this week. We would like you to come to play for us. We have practices on Tuesday, Wednesday, and Friday from 7:00 p.m. to 9:00 p.m. We practice at the Springfield Community Center, in Room 208. Which is the best day for you? After all three people have played for us, we'll invite one person. You can listen to our music on our website. The address is www.springfieldfive.com.
Dan

From: Melanie Jones
To: Dan Campbell
Date: October 1
Subject: Great music

Dear Dan,
I think your music is great. I'd like to come on Wednesday. I've been practicing a song called "Maybe Tomorrow." It's a song that I wrote myself. I hope you like it. I'm excited to meet you and the other members of your band.
Melanie

(1) When did Melanie come to Springfield?
1 Yesterday.
2 Five years ago.
3 Last Sunday.
4 One month ago.

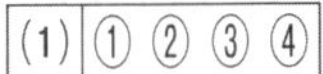

(2) What does Melanie want to do?
1 Join Dan's band.
2 Get tickets to Dan's concert.
3 Sell her guitar to Dan.
4 Work at Dan's music store.

(3) What will Melanie do next Wednesday?
1 Go to the Springfield Community Center.
2 Write a new song.
3 Practice for her concert.
4 Make a new design for Dan's website.

 ⇒本冊 p.96 ~ 107

DATA
●ワード数：248 words
●目標解答時間：15 分

Read the passage and choose the best answer from among the four choices for each question. Then, on your answer sheet, find the number of the question and mark your answer.

Annie Londonderry

In June 1894, an American woman named Annie Londonderry started a long trip. She said goodbye to her husband and children in Boston and started riding her bicycle. Her plan was to ride it all around North America, Europe, and Asia, and return to Boston. It was a round-the-world trip*!

At first, Londonderry rode a very heavy bicycle. It was more than 20 kilograms. She could only ride about 12 to 15 kilometers each day. She thought about ending her trip. But then in Chicago, she got a lighter bicycle. It was only 10 kilograms. After that, she could ride much faster.

Londonderry took a boat from New York to France. She had many problems in France. First, someone stole her money. The weather was also very bad. Finally, she hurt her foot. She needed more money. She asked companies to pay her to put their names on signs on her bicycle. She showed things like bicycle tires and perfume.

Londonderry traveled across Europe and Asia, and she returned to Chicago in 1895. She became famous and got a lot of money. She also told many stories about her trip. She fought in a war in China and killed tigers in Asia. Many of her stories were not true, but she still did a great thing. She traveled around the world. In those days, many people thought women were weaker than men. But she showed people that women could do anything that men could do.

*a round-the-world trip: 世界一周旅行

(1) What was Annie Londonderry's plan?

1 To make a new kind of bicycle.
2 To take a vacation with her family.
3 To teach people in other countries about Boston.
4 To travel around the world.

(1) ① ② ③ ④

(2) After Londonderry left Chicago,

1 she could ride faster.
2 she lost 20 kilograms.
3 she stopped her trip.
4 she went to Boston.

(2) ① ② ③ ④

(3) Londonderry got money by

1 stealing from people in France.
2 selling her bicycle tires.
3 putting signs on her bicycle.
4 carrying things like perfume.

(4) After Londonderry's trip ended,

1 she went to China again.
2 she showed people the tigers she killed.
3 she told some stories about it.
4 she gave away a lot of money.

(5) Londonderry showed people that

1 American bicycles were the best.
2 women could do the same things as men.
3 heavy bicycles were better than light ones.
4 tigers in Asia were dangerous.

(5) ① ② ③ ④

 ⇒本冊 p.108 ~ 119

DATA
●ワード数：270 words
●目標解答時間：15 分

Read the passage and choose the best answer from among the four choices for each question. Then, on your answer sheet, find the number of the question and mark your answer.

The Bathtub Race

Nanaimo is a small city near Vancouver in Canada. In 1967, Canada was 100 years old. People in Nanaimo decided to hold a special event to celebrate Canada's birthday. They made a funny kind of race. They asked people to put motors on bathtubs and see who could go the fastest in them. It was called the Great International World Championship Bathtub Race.

There were around 200 bathtubs in the first race. Nanaimo is on an island, and the bathtubs had to go about 58 kilometers across the sea to the city of Vancouver. Bathtubs are heavy, and they are not made to go in the sea. Only 47 of them finished the race. The others needed to be rescued by people in boats. The first winner was a man named Rusty Harrison.

One of the most famous racers was a man named Frank Ney. He helped to start the first race in Nanaimo, and he was also the city's mayor*. He loved boats, and he often dressed like a pirate* when he was racing. He never won, but he had a lot of fun. He also liked the race because it brought many tourists to Nanaimo.

The bathtubs used in the first race were real bathtubs. But in the 1970s, some Australian people started coming to Nanaimo for the race. They used bathtubs made of fiberglass*. They were lighter, so they were faster. People also started using bigger motors. In 1967, the first place finisher won the race in three hours and 26 minutes. In 2016, the best time was just one hour and seven minutes.

*mayor: 市長
*pirate: 海賊（かいぞく）
*fiberglass: ガラス繊維（せんい），グラスファイバー

(1) Why did the bathtub race start?

1 To test new boat motors.
2 To sell a new kind of bathtub.
3 To try to cross the ocean with a bathtub.
4 To celebrate Canada's birthday.

(1)	① ② ③ ④

(2) How many boats finished the first race?

1 47.
2 57.
3 100.
4 200.

(2)	① ② ③ ④

(3) Frank Ney was

1 a famous pirate.
2 a mayor of Nanaimo.
3 a tourist who loved the race.
4 a boat maker.

(3)	① ② ③ ④

(4) In the 1970s,

1 the race became longer.
2 the bathtubs became faster.
3 the race moved to Australia.
4 the bathtubs were made bigger.

(4)	① ② ③ ④

(5) This story is about

1 the history of bathtubs.
2 a funny kind of race.
3 the life of Rusty Harrison.
4 a new kind of motor.

(5)	① ② ③ ④

⇒本冊 p.120 ~ 131

DATA
●ワード数：271 words
●目標解答時間：15 分

Read the passage and choose the best answer from among the four choices for each question. Then, on your answer sheet, find the number of the question and mark your answer.

Bobbie the Wonder Dog

In August 1923, the Brazier family went on vacation. They lived in Silverton, Oregon, but they drove to Wolcott, Indiana, to visit their relatives*. Oregon is on the west side of America, but Indiana is on the east side. Silverton is about 4,100 kilometers from Wolcott. The family took their dog, Bobbie, but something terrible happened. Bobbie was attacked by three other dogs. He ran away very quickly.

The Braziers drove all around Wolcott. They asked people for information about their big brown and white dog. They even put an advertisement* in the newspaper. But no one saw Bobbie. After a few days, they had to go home without Bobbie. Six months later, in February 1924, the Brazier family was in the café that they owned. They were very surprised because Bobbie walked into the café.

Bobbie came all the way from Wolcott to Silverton. He swam across wide rivers and walked through snowstorms*. On the way, Bobbie had an accident and hurt his legs badly. In Portland, he stayed with a woman who gave him food and put bandages* on his legs. He traveled 4,100 kilometers, and he was very thin. The Braziers gave him a big steak and had a party to welcome him home.

In 1924, the Silverton newspaper wrote a story about Bobbie's trip. Other newspapers saw the story, and Bobbie became famous all over America. A book was written about Bobbie, and then a movie was made about him, too. Bobbie played himself in it! When Bobbie got sick and died in 1927, hundreds of people came to say goodbye to him.

*relative: 親戚（しんせき）
*put an advertisement: 広告を出す
*snowstorm: 吹雪（ふぶき）
*bandage: 包帯

(1) What happened during the Brazier family's trip to Indiana?

1 The Braziers got lost while driving.

2 The Braziers got three new dogs.

3 Bobbie ran away.

4 Bobbie did not like the Braziers' relatives.

(1) ① ② ③ ④

(2) What happened in February 1924?

1 Bobbie was found by people in Wolcott.

2 Bobbie came into the Braziers' café.

3 The Braziers put an advertisement in the newspaper.

4 The Braziers got a new black and white dog.

(3) Where did someone put bandages on Bobbie's legs?

1 In Wolcott.

2 In Silverton.

3 In Portland.

4 In Indiana.

(4) What happened after Bobbie came home?

1 Bobbie was in a movie.

2 Bobbie traveled all over America.

3 The Braziers wrote a book about him.

4 The Braziers became sick.

(5) This story is about

1 a famous café.

2 a race for dogs.

3 a family that had many dogs.

4 a dog that traveled very far.

(5) ① ② ③ ④

Unit 14

⇒本冊 p.132 ~ 143

DATA
●ワード数：280 words
●目標解答時間：15 分

Read the passage and choose the best answer from among the four choices for each question. Then, on your answer sheet, find the number of the question and mark your answer.

The Burj Al Arab

Dubai is one of the world's richest cities and has many expensive hotels. The most luxurious* one is the Burj Al Arab. Many guidebooks give stars to hotels. A cheap, simple hotel gets just one star, and the best hotels in the world get five stars. But some people say that is not enough for the Burj Al Arab. They say it should get seven stars.

Workers started building the Burj Al Arab in 1994. First, they built an island in the ocean. It took three years. Then, work on the hotel building started in 1997. More than 2,000 people worked on it every day. It was finally completed* in 1999. Many people say the building is beautiful because it looks like the sail of a boat.

When guests go to hotels from the airport, they usually take a bus or train. However, most of the Burj Al Arab's guests are picked up in a Rolls Royce. A Rolls Royce is one of the most expensive cars in the world. When guests arrive at their room, there is a butler*. This is a person who does everything for the guests. The butler even takes their clothes out of the suitcase and gets a bath ready for them. Guests can call the butler 24 hours a day.

The hotel costs a lot of money, and it wants its guests to feel special when they stay there. Guests are given many choices. For example, there is a menu with 17 different kinds of pillows* for guests to choose from. Also, there is gold on the walls and the chairs, and guests can borrow an iPad made of gold.

*luxurious: 豪華（ごうか）な
*complete: 完成させる
*butler: 執事
*pillow: 枕（まくら）

(1) People say the Burj Al Arab is

1 the largest hotel in the world.
2 cheaper than other hotels in Dubai.
3 a hotel that is not in guidebooks.
4 a seven-star hotel.

(1) ① ② ③ ④

(2) When was the Burj Al Arab finished?

1 In 1994.
2 In 1997.
3 In 1999.
4 In 2000.

(3) Most guests at the Burj Al Arab

1 get free suitcases.
2 can ride on a high-speed train.
3 arrive there in an expensive car.
4 take baths at other hotels.

(3) ① ② ③ ④

(4) Guests at the Burj Al Arab feel special because

1 they can take home a free iPad.
2 they get gold as a present.
3 they can choose from many different things.
4 the pillows have gold in them.

(4) ① ② ③ ④

(5) This story is about

1 a new kind of boat.
2 an expensive hotel.
3 an airport in Dubai.
4 people who work in hotels.

(5) ① ② ③ ④

⇒本冊 p.144 ~ 155

DATA
●ワード数：241 words
●目標解答時間：15 分

Read the passage and choose the best answer from among the four choices for each question. Then, on your answer sheet, find the number of the question and mark your answer.

Cliff Young

In Australia, there was a famous race called the Westfield Sydney to Melbourne Ultramarathon. It started in 1983. A marathon is about 42 kilometers long, but this race was much longer. It was 875 kilometers, and it took six or seven days to finish.

Most of the people in the race were famous runners. But one man was different. His name was Cliff Young. He was 61 years old. He was not a runner. He was a farmer. The other runners were under 30. No one thought that Young could win. Some people were worried that he might get sick or die.

There was something that no one knew about Young. He had a lot of sheep on his farm. He was poor, and he did not have a horse or a car. He had to chase* the sheep. Sometimes, he chased the sheep for three days. It was good practice for the ultramarathon.

Young was much slower than the other runners. After running for about 18 hours, the runners stopped to sleep. They slept for about six hours. But Young's coach set his alarm clock too early by mistake. Young started running after sleeping for two hours. After that, he did not sleep much. While the other runners were sleeping, he kept running. He won the race. He also made a new record* of five days, fifteen hours, and four minutes. He became famous all over the world.

*chase: 追う
*record: 記録

(1) How long was the Sydney to Melbourne Ultramarathon?

1 42 kilometers.

2 61 kilometers.

3 875 kilometers.

4 1983 kilometers.

(1) ① ② ③ ④

(2) How was Cliff Young different from the other runners?

1 He was much older.

2 He was more famous.

3 He had more experience.

4 He was very sick.

(2) ① ② ③ ④

(3) How did Young become a good runner?

1 He trained behind a car.

2 He ran beside a horse.

3 He ran after sheep.

4 He traveled around Australia.

(3) ① ② ③ ④

(4) What did Young's coach do?

1 He woke Young up too early.

2 He told Young to sleep more.

3 He talked to the other runners.

4 He fell asleep by mistake.

(4) ① ② ③ ④

(5) This story is about

1 a farmer who became a famous runner.

2 30 famous runners.

3 a race between a man and a horse.

4 a sleeping contest.

(5) ① ② ③ ④

 ⇒本冊 p.156 ~ 167

DATA
●ワード数：264 words
●目標解答時間：15 分

Read the passage and choose the best answer from among the four choices for each question. Then, on your answer sheet, find the number of the question and mark your answer.

Curiosity

Humans can't live on Mars* easily. There is no air, and it is too cold. But people want to know about Mars. In November 2011, a rocket was sent to Mars. Inside the rocket was a robot named Curiosity. Its job was to learn about the environment* and look for elements* necessary to support life. It traveled through space and arrived on Mars in August 2012.

When Curiosity left the rocket and went down to Mars from space, scientists were worried. Curiosity was expensive, and they were worried it could break. Curiosity had to fall down from the sky. They used a special parachute and small rockets to slow it down. Everyone was happy when it landed safely.

Curiosity has six wheels, and it is 2.9 meters long and 2.7 meters wide. It moves slowly, but it can do many things. It has 17 cameras. They take pictures and send them back to Earth. Curiosity also has a two-meter-long arm. It can pick up rocks and other things. The arm has a drill, so Curiosity can study things which are under the ground.

Scientists thought Curiosity could only be used for two years. But Curiosity has now been on Mars for more than six years. It probably has enough power to work for 15 years. It was also built with many things it might not need. It has a backup* computer because the main computer may break. Also, it does not need all six wheels to move around. Scientists think that Curiosity will be able to travel around Mars for a long time.

*Mars: 火星
*environment: 環境
*element: 要素
*backup: 予備の

(1) What happened in August 2012?

1 Mars became colder.

2 A robot arrived on Mars.

3 Scientists found life on Mars.

4 Scientists made a new kind of rocket.

(1) ① ② ③ ④

(2) Why were the scientists worried?

1 Curiosity's parachute was too small.

2 They thought Curiosity might break.

3 Curiosity's rockets were too slow.

4 The rocket carrying Curiosity broke.

(3) Curiosity can

1 move very fast.

2 bring rocks back to Earth.

3 find things under the ground.

4 become longer or wider.

(3) ① ② ③ ④

(4) Scientists think that

1 Curiosity's computer is broken.

2 Curiosity can be used for a long time.

3 Curiosity does not have enough power.

4 Curiosity needs new wheels.

(5) What is this story about?

1 The history of rockets.

2 Sending humans to Mars.

3 A robot working on Mars.

4 Making a building on Mars.

(5) ① ② ③ ④

⇒本冊 p.168 ~ 179

DATA
●ワード数：261 words
●目標解答時間：15 分

Read the passage and choose the best answer from among the four choices for each question. Then, on your answer sheet, find the number of the question and mark your answer.

The Dakar

In 1977, a French man named Thierry Sabine went to Libya to ride his motorcycle. Riding in the desert* was very dangerous, and he got lost. But it was also beautiful and exciting. He decided to make a new kind of race called the Dakar Rally. He wanted it to be the world's most difficult race. The drivers had to travel from the city of Paris in France to Dakar in the African country of Senegal.

The first race was in 1978. At the beginning, there were 170 teams in the race. The drivers did not usually drive on roads. They drove on sand, grass, and gravel*. Many of the racers got hurt, and some of their cars and motorcycles were damaged. Only 74 teams were able to finish the race. In 2018, 335 teams started the race and 246 finished.

For many years, the Dakar Rally was held in Africa. The race was usually about 10,000 kilometers long and went through six or more countries. But people became worried that Africa was too dangerous. They were worried about terrorism*. Because of that, the race went to South America in 2009. This time, it went through Argentina and Chile.

People sometimes say that too many racers get hurt in the Dakar Rally. More than 70 people have died, and some people say it should be safer. Now, helicopters watch the racers, and there are many doctors and nurses to help people who get hurt. Also, the cars and motorcycles are becoming safer. But it is still a dangerous race.

*desert: 砂漠（さばく）
*gravel: 砂利（じゃり）
*terrorism: テロ行為

(1) In 1977, Thierry Sabine

1 got lost in the desert.

2 traveled around the world.

3 drove over 9,000 kilometers.

4 made a new kind of motorcycle.

(1) ① ② ③ ④

(2) How many teams finished the Dakar Rally in 1978?

1 74.

2 170.

3 246.

4 335.

(2) ① ② ③ ④

(3) What happened to the Dakar Rally in 2009?

1 It became much longer.

2 It became more dangerous.

3 It started going through six countries.

4 It moved to South America.

(3) ① ② ③ ④

(4) What do some people say about the Dakar Rally?

1 The helicopters are too slow.

2 Different cars should be used.

3 It needs more doctors and nurses.

4 It is too dangerous.

(5) This story is about

1 a city in Africa.

2 a very long race.

3 a man who lost his motorcycle.

4 a new kind of motorcycle.

(5) ① ② ③ ④

⇒本冊 p.180 ~ 191

DATA
●ワード数：266 words
●目標解答時間：15 分

Read the passage and choose the best answer from among the four choices for each question. Then, on your answer sheet, find the number of the question and mark your answer.

Davy Crockett

Davy Crockett was born in the United States in 1786. His parents had nine children, so it was hard to get food for everyone. He learned how to shoot a gun* when he was just eight years old so he could kill animals for food. When he was 12, he helped to take cows on a 600-kilometer trip. When Crockett was 14, his father wanted him to go to school. Crockett did not like it, so he left home.

Crockett loved to be in the forest, and he knew a lot about animals. A long time ago, many people ate bear meat. Also, people did not have electricity, so they made candles from bear fat. Bears were dangerous animals, but it was important to hunt them for food and safety. In one year, Crockett killed 105 of these animals. That made him very famous.

Later, Crockett went to Texas. Today, Texas is a state in America. But in those days, Texas was part of Mexico. People in Texas did not like Mexico. They wanted Texas to be free. Crockett went and fought with them. He was in a battle at a church called the Alamo in 1836. He died, but the battle became famous because the people were fighting to be free.

In the 1950s, a TV show was made about Crockett. The show became one of the world's most famous TV shows. In the show, Crockett wore a special hat called a "coonskin cap*." It was made of raccoon fur*. Millions of children wanted to look like Crockett, so they bought these hats.

*shoot a gun: 銃(じゅう)を撃つ
*coonskin cap: クーンスキンキャップ（アライグマのしっぽ付き帽子）
*raccoon fur: アライグマの毛皮

(1) Davy Crockett left home when he was

1 eight.
2 nine.
3 twelve.
4 fourteen.

(1)	① ② ③ ④

(2) Crockett became famous because he

1 killed many bears.
2 made a new kind of candle.
3 taught people about nature.
4 found a new kind of animal.

(2)	① ② ③ ④

(3) What happened to Crockett in 1836?

1 He started a new church.
2 He taught people about Mexico.
3 He wrote a book about Texas.
4 He died in a battle.

(3)	① ② ③ ④

(4) In the 1950s, many children

1 bought coonskin caps.
2 had pet raccoons.
3 studied about Crockett in school.
4 read books about Crockett.

(4)	① ② ③ ④

(5) This story is about

1 an actor in a famous TV show.
2 a famous hat maker.
3 a man who had many adventures.
4 the history of Mexico.

(5)	① ② ③ ④

 ⇒本冊 p.192 ~ 203

DATA
●ワード数：256 words
●目標解答時間：15 分

Read the passage and choose the best answer from among the four choices for each question. Then, on your answer sheet, find the number of the question and mark your answer.

Death Valley

Death Valley is a desert in America. It is the hottest place on Earth. In July in Death Valley, it is over 40°C almost every day. Death Valley also had the hottest day in the history of the world on July 10, 1913. It was 56°C. People say the best time to visit is in February. It is not so hot, and there are many flowers then.

There are more than 900 kinds of plants in Death Valley. One is a very small tree called mesquite*. Death Valley usually gets only about 5 cm of rain in a year. But mesquite has very long roots*. They can go down more than 15 meters into the ground. They bring water up to the plant.

There are also many animals. Bighorn sheep* can live without water for over a month. Kangaroo rats* sleep all day and only come out at night. And kangaroo rats sometimes do not drink water at all. Kangaroo rats get most of the water they need from the air and from eating seeds* and plants.

People called the Timbisha Shoshone* have lived in Death Valley for over a thousand years. In the 1800s, some American pioneers* went there. They thought Death Valley was hot and scary. The Timbisha Shoshone knew how to find water, but the pioneers did not. Some of the pioneers died, so they called it "Death Valley." But the Timbisha Shoshone do not like that name. Death Valley is their home, and they don't want to live anywhere else.

*mesquite: メスキート
*root: 根
*bighorn sheep: オオツノヒツジ
*kangaroo rat: カンガルーネズミ
*seed: 種
*Timbisha Shoshone: ティンビシャ・ショショーニ族
*pioneer: 開拓者

(1) In Death Valley in the month of February,

1 it is usually over 40°C.

2 you can see flowers.

3 it is the hottest time of the year.

4 there is rain every day.

(1)	① ② ③ ④

(2) The mesquite tree

1 can live more than 900 years.

2 can get water from under the ground.

3 has the largest leaves in the world.

4 grows 5 cm every day.

(2)	① ② ③ ④

(3) When do kangaroo rats drink water?

1 Once a month.

2 Twice a day.

3 Only at night.

4 Almost never.

(3)	① ② ③ ④

(4) The Timbisha Shoshone

1 do not like the name Death Valley.

2 think Death Valley is hot and scary.

3 helped the pioneers find water.

4 want to leave Death Valley.

(4)	① ② ③ ④

(5) This story is about

1 a dangerous plant.

2 why plants need water.

3 an American animal.

4 the hottest place in the world.

(5)	① ② ③ ④

⇒本冊 p.204 ~ 215

DATA
●ワード数：256 words
●目標解答時間：15 分

Read the passage and choose the best answer from among the four choices for each question. Then, on your answer sheet, find the number of the question and mark your answer.

Ellen MacArthur

In 1980, when Ellen MacArthur was four years old, her aunt took her sailing. She loved it, and she wanted to do it every day, but she had a problem. She and her parents lived in a place called Derbyshire in England. It is far from the ocean. She started reading many books about sailing and dreamed about having her own boat.

When MacArthur was 10, she started saving money. She bought cheap clothes and cheap food so she could get money for a boat. Finally, in 1995, when she was 17, she had enough money to get one. That same year, she sailed her new boat all around the country.

In 2001, MacArthur entered the Vendée Globe*. It is a race around the world. She did not win, but people were surprised that a young woman could sail around the world alone on her first try. She was only 24. In 2005, she sailed around the world again. This time, she set a world record. She made the trip in just 71 days.

MacArthur became very famous. She was young, and people thought she would keep racing. But she wanted to do something different. One day, while she was sailing, she saw birds being killed. She wanted to stop people from hurting nature. She stopped racing. She started a group called the Ellen MacArthur Foundation* in 2009. It teaches people to recycle. She was a great racer and a great sailor, but now she is working hard to make Earth a better place.

*Vendée Globe: ヴァンデ・グローブ（単独無寄港無補給世界一周ヨットレース）
*Ellen MacArthur Foundation: エレン・マッカーサー財団

(1) What was Ellen MacArthur's problem?

1 She lived far from the ocean.

2 She could not get sailing books.

3 Her aunt's boat was not safe.

4 Her parents did not like sailing.

(1) ① ② ③ ④

(2) When MacArthur was 17 years old, she

1 went sailing for the first time.

2 started saving her money.

3 bought a book about sailing.

4 sailed her boat around England.

(2) ① ② ③ ④

(3) When did MacArthur sail around the world the first time?

1 In 1980.

2 In 1995.

3 In 2001.

4 In 2005.

(3) ① ② ③ ④

(4) Today, Ellen MacArthur

1 has a group that teaches people to recycle.

2 goes in sailing races every year.

3 studies birds while sailing.

4 teaches young people about sailing.

(4) ① ② ③ ④

(5) This story is about

1 a writer of sailing stories.

2 a woman who is good at sailing.

3 a woman who made a new kind of boat.

4 a scientist who studies seabirds.

(5) ① ② ③ ④

桐原書店

978-4-342-20581-1

英語4技能
リーディング
ハイパートレーニング

東進ハイスクール講師 安河内哲也
ハーバード大学
教育学大学院修士 アンドリュー・ロビンス［監修］

長文読解 2 基礎編

桐原書店

はじめに

本書は4技能のうち，リーディング力を高めることを主目的としています。**さらに，音声を活用してリーディングを学ぶことにより，同時にリスニングの力をのばす**ことを狙（ねら）います。

リーディングとリスニングを融合（ゆうごう）して学習することには多くの利点があります。耳と口と目をフル活用して英語を学ぶことで，相互に助け合いそれぞれの技能を支え合うのです。たとえば，音声を耳で聞いて，口を動かしながら読むことによって，英語をそのまま左から右へと理解する最高の読解訓練ができます。また，学習が終了し，理解できるようになった英文を耳で聞くことにより，語い，表現，内容を保持するための復習が容易にできるわけです。

このように，リーディングをリスニングと組み合わせて学ぶことにより，学習効果は何倍にもなります。4技能の英語をマスターするためには，4技能を別々に学ぶのではなく，極力融合して学ぶことが大切なのです。

本書で訓練するリーディングの内容や語いは，スピーキングやライティングのネタとしても使えるでしょう。このように，内容を4技能で使い回しすることにより，将来も役に立つスピード感のある英語力を，皆さんが身につけることを願います。

安河内 哲也

本書の内容と使い方

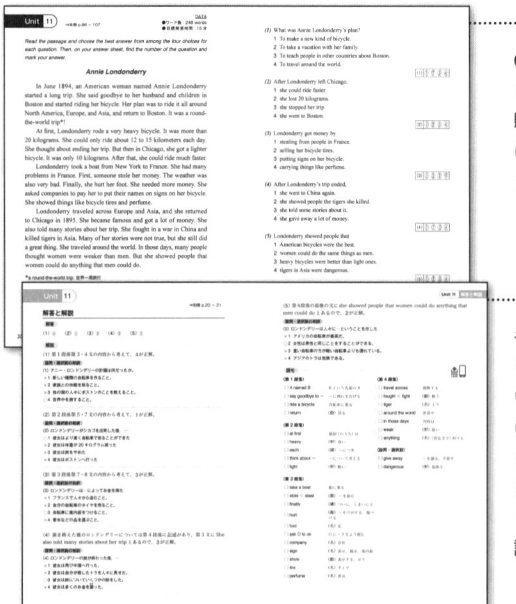
Unit 11 →本冊 p.96 ~ 107

DATA
●ワード数：248 words
●目標解答時間：15 分

Read the passage and choose the best answer from among the four choices for each question. Then, on your answer sheet, find the number of the question and mark your answer.

Annie Londonderry

In June 1894, an American woman named Annie Londonderry started a long trip. She said goodbye to her husband and children in Boston and started riding her bicycle. Her plan was to ride it all around North America, Europe, and Asia, and return to Boston. It was a round-the-world trip*!

At first, Londonderry rode a very heavy bicycle. It was more than 20 kilograms. She could only ride about 12 to 15 kilometers each day. She thought about ending her trip. But then in Chicago, she got a lighter bicycle. It was only 10 kilograms. After that, she could ride much faster.

Londonderry took a boat from New York to France. She had many problems in France. First, someone stole her money. The weather was also very bad. Finally, she hurt her foot. She needed more money. She asked companies to pay her to put their names on signs on her bicycle. She showed things like bicycle tires and perfume.

Londonderry traveled across Europe and Asia, and she returned to Chicago in 1895. She became famous and got a lot of money. She also told many stories about her trip. She fought in a war in China and killed tigers in Asia. Many of her stories were not true, but she still did a great thing. She traveled around the world. In those days, many people thought women were weaker than men. But she showed people that women could do anything that men could do.

*a round-the-world trip: 世界一周旅行

(1) What was Annie Londonderry's plan?
1 To make a new kind of bicycle.
2 To take a vacation with her family.
3 To teach people in other countries about Boston.
4 To travel around the world.

(2) After Londonderry left Chicago,
1 she could ride faster.
2 she lost 20 kilograms.
3 she stopped her trip.
4 she went to Boston.

(3) Londonderry got money by
1 stealing from people in France.
2 selling her bicycle tires.
3 putting signs on her bicycle.
4 carrying things like perfume.

(4) After Londonderry's trip ended,
1 she went to China again.
2 she showed people the tigers she killed.
3 she told some stories about it.
4 she gave away a lot of money.

(5) Londonderry showed people that
1 American bicycles were the best.
2 women could do the same things as men.
3 heavy bicycles were better than light ones.
4 tigers in Asia were dangerous.

Unit 11 →別冊 p.20 ~ 21

解答と解説

問題（別冊）

CEFRと英検®のレベルに準拠して作成された問題です。設問は，どのような試験にでも応用できる力を身につけるために，英問英答問題を中心としたオーソドックスなものとしています。

解答と解説

各設問について，対応する部分などを示し，解答の根拠をわかりやすく説明しています。解説を読み，どう考えれば正解に至ることができるのかを理解してください。

また，語句は長文の中で学んで覚えていくのが最良の勉強方法です。本書には単語集としての機能も持たせてあります。

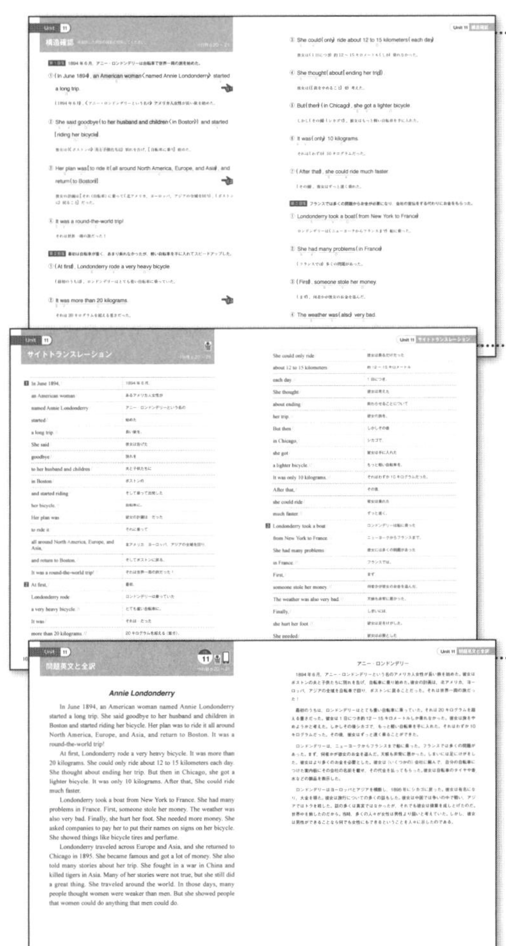
Unit 11 構造確認

Unit 11 サイトトランスレーション

Unit 11 問題英文と全訳

Annie Londonderry

In June 1894, an American woman named Annie Londonderry started a long trip. She said goodbye to her husband and children in Boston and started riding her bicycle. Her plan was to ride it all around North America, Europe, and Asia, and return to Boston. It was a round-the-world trip!

At first, Londonderry rode a very heavy bicycle. It was more than 20 kilograms. She could only ride about 12 to 15 kilometers each day. She thought about ending her trip. But then in Chicago, she got a lighter bicycle. It was only 10 kilograms. After that, She could ride much faster.

Londonderry took a boat from New York to France. She had many problems in France. First, someone stole her money. The weather was also very bad. Finally, she hurt her foot. She needed more money. She asked companies to pay her to put their names on signs on her bicycle. She showed things like bicycle tires and perfume.

Londonderry traveled across Europe and Asia, and she returned to Chicago in 1895. She became famous and got a lot of money. She also told many stories about her trip. She fought in a war in China and killed tigers in Asia. Many of her stories were not true, but she still did a great thing. She traveled around the world. In those days, many people thought women were weaker than men. But she showed people that women could do anything that men could do.

106

107

構造確認

各文章の構造を，記号やSVOCを付し，確認できるようにしました（くわしくはp.6～7を参照）。あくまでも読み違えたときの確認のためのものであり，自分でこのような作業をすることを求めるものではありません。

サイトトランスレーション

英文をチャンク（かたまり）ごとに分け，英語と日本語を左右に分けて編集することにより，英文を前から読むためのさまざまな練習を可能としました。後置修飾部分も「後から説明」と考えながら，前からすばやく英文を処理する練習をしてください。最終的には，日本語を見ずに英語が理解できることを目指しましょう。

問題英文と全訳

和訳は英文を読む目的ではありませんが，読み違えがないかどうかの確認には便利です。その用途を意識し，本書ではできるだけ構造に忠実な和訳を心がけています。

本書に準拠した音声と練習用動画に関して

本書の英文を使って，チャンクリピーティング，オーバーラッピング，シャドウイング，リスニングなどの練習ができるダウンロード音声と動画が準備されています。皆さんは，これらの音声や動画の画面を使って以下のような基礎訓練をし，リーディング力とリスニング力を向上させてください。

【チャンクリピーティング】

チャンクごとに分けて読まれる英語の後に続けて，本や画面の文字を見ながら，英文を音読しましょう。また，このようにして，文字を見ながら英文の意味が理解できるようになったら，次は本や画面の文字を見ないで，音だけでリピートしながら意味を理解する訓練をしてみましょう。

【オーバーラッピング】

テキストや画面の文字を見ながら，ネイティブスピーカーと一緒（いっしょ）に音読してみましょう。その際，音だけに集中しすぎず，英文の意味を理解しようと努めましょう。

【シャドウイング】

ネイティブスピーカーの音声から一拍遅れながら，耳だけでネイティブスピーカーの音声をまねてみましょう。非常に難しい訓練なので，できなくても心配する必要はまったくありませんが，一つの目標としてチャレンジしてみてください。

【リスニング】

本や画面の文字を見ずに，英語だけを聞いて意味が理解できるか確認してみてください。100％理解できたら，その英文をマスターしたと言えるでしょう。その後も復習として，ラジオを聞く感覚で，文章を耳で聞いて，内容，語い，表現を忘れないようにしましょう。

本書の英文に関して

本シリーズの英文は，アンドリュー・ロビンス氏の監修のもと，作成されています。本書では，ロビンス氏が，日米のネイティブスピーカーのアイテムライターをチーム化し，英語学習者が力をのばすのにふさわしいレベルの多くの英文をプロデュースしました。本書の英文は，CEFR（ヨーロッパ言語共通参照枠（わく））という国際的言語教育の枠組みに準拠して作成されています。

この目的を達成するために，ロビンス氏は，語いレベルや構造レベルを色分けし，直感的なフィードバックを与えるソフトウェアを開発しました。このソフトウェアでは，一般に公表されている CEFR-J※の語いリストや，CEFR との準拠を公表している英検®などの，4 技能試験で出題頻度（ひんど）の高い語いを色別表示することができます。このことにより，アイテムライターは，使用している語いが当該（とうがい）の CEFR レベルにマッチするものなのかをつねに確認しながらライティング作業を進めることができるようになりました。

しかしながら，このような機械によるアルゴリズム分析（ぶんせき）には大きな限界があります。それは，機械の判断では，文脈からの意味判定が非常に難しいということです。たとえば，free という形容詞が「自由な」という意味で使用された場合，CEFR-J では A1 のレベルですが，「ない」という意味で使用されている場合は，より高いレベルに分類されると考えられます。

また，内容の選択に関しても，機械分析には限界があります。特定の予備知識を持っていなければ理解できないような素材は，基礎から学んでいる学生の学習素材として適しているとは言えません。そこで本書では，内容選択においても各種 4 技能試験に準拠し，一般的，基礎的な常識を備えていれば読めるものを選択しています。

このように，本書の英文は，機械分析と熟練した編著者，アイテムライターを組み合わせ，CEFR レベルの準拠と等価を行い，ロビンス氏の監修のもとで作成されました。

※ CEFR-J：実質上の国際標準となっている CEFR を，日本のような環境に適合させるために開発された枠組み。レベル別の語いリストが一般に公表されている。

もくじ

構造確認について

構造確認のページは，誤読が生じた場合にその原因を確認するためのものです。ただし，５文型や句や節の分類には何通りもの解釈があり，本書ではその一つを示しているにすぎません。これらの記号を使えなければならないということを意味しているわけではないので，このページを詳細に学習する必要はありません。あくまでも，誤読しないための参考資料として使用するにとどめてください。

使用されている記号一覧

主文［主節］の構造：S＝主語　V＝動詞　O＝目的語　C＝補語

主文［主節］以外の構造：S'＝主語　V'＝動詞　O'＝目的語　C'＝補語

[　]→ 名詞の働きをするもの（名詞，名詞句，名詞節）

〈　〉→ 形容詞の働きをするもの（形容詞，形容詞句，形容詞節）

(　)→ 副詞の働きをするもの（副詞，副詞句，副詞節）

〈　〉→ 形容詞の働きをするものが，後ろから名詞を修飾

名詞の働きをするもの

●動名詞

I like [watching baseball games].

私は［野球を見ること］が好きだ。

●不定詞の名詞的用法

[To see] is [to believe].

［見ること］は［信じること］である。

●疑問詞＋不定詞

I don't know [what to do next].

私は［次に何をすべきか］わからない。

●that 節「S が V するということ」

I think [that he is right].

私は［彼は正しい］と思う。

●疑問詞節

Do you know [where he lives]?

あなたは［彼がどこに住んでいるか］知っていますか。

形容詞の働きをするもの

● 前置詞＋名詞

Look at the girl 〈in a white dress〉.

〈白い服を着た〉女の子を見てごらん。

● 不定詞の形容詞的用法

I have many friends 〈to help me〉.

私は〈私を助けてくれる〉たくさんの友人がいる。

● 現在分詞

Look at the building 〈standing on that hill〉.

〈あの丘の上に建っている〉建物を見なさい。

● 過去分詞

The car carried a child 〈hit by a truck〉.

その車は〈トラックにはねられた〉子供を運んだ。

● 関係代名詞節

He is the boy 〈who broke the window〉.

彼が〈窓を壊した〉少年だ。

同格の働きをするもの

※名詞に接続する同格節［句］は本来，名詞の働きをするものですが，本書では英文を理解しやすくするために，あえて〈 〉記号にしてあります。

● 同格の that 節

There is some hope 〈that he will win the race〉.

〈彼がそのレースに勝つという〉いくぶんの希望がある。

● カンマによる同格補足

We visited Osaka, 〈the big city in Japan〉.

私たちは〈日本の大都市である〉大阪を訪れた。

副詞の働きをするもの

● 前置詞＋名詞

The sun rises (in the east).

太陽は（東から）のぼる。

● 不定詞の副詞的用法

I was very glad (to hear the news).

私は（その知らせを聞いて）とてもうれしい。

● 従属接続詞＋ＳＶ

I went to bed early (because I was tired).

（私は疲れていたので）早く寝た。

サイトトランスレーションについて ―センスグループの分け方―

スラッシュなどで英文を区切るセンスグループの分け方には，明確なルールがあるわけではありませんが，基本的には２～５語ほどの「意味のかたまり」でリズムよく分けていきます。大切なのは，「切る」という作業が目標になってしまわないことです。皆さんの目標は「読んでわかる」ことであり，切り方ばかりに集中するあまり，読むのが遅くなってしまっては本末転倒です。最初はおおざっぱに切り分けてどんどん読んでいき，徐々(じょじょ)に文法を意識した正確な切り方を覚えていきましょう。

SVOC の要素で切る

S，V，O，C は文の最も基本的な要素なので，これらはセンスグループを切り分ける際にも非常に重要なヒントとなります。1つの要素が4語や5語のような大きなものになる場合は，それを1つのセンスグループとするとよいでしょう。

He told me / a very interesting story.
S V O　　O
彼は私に語った / とても興味深い話を

文頭の副詞や副詞句の後ろで切る

文頭に副詞や副詞句が置かれる場合は，それらの副詞句と主語の間では必ず切って読み進みましょう。文頭で副詞句の働きをするものとしては，前置詞句などが考えられます。

Because of the fire, / we couldn't go home.
前置詞句　S V
その火事のせいで / 私たちは帰れなかった。

長い主語の後ろで切る

主語の直後に長い修飾部分が続く場合は，その主語と述語動詞を切り分けて読むことが重要です。通常一拍おいて読まれ，少々強い切れ目となります。

The songs / that she made / were great.
主語　+関係代名詞節　述部
曲は / 彼女が作った / すばらしかった。

前置詞や接続詞の前で切る

前置詞や接続詞は直後に続く語句と結びついてかたまりを作るため，多くの場合その直前で切って読みます。前置詞とその目的語の間で切ることはまずありません。

He stayed / in the house / during the afternoon.
S V　前置詞句　前置詞句
彼はとどまった / 家の中に / 午後の間は

I like him / because he is kind and smart.
主節　接続詞＋SV（副詞節）
私は彼が好きだ / なぜなら彼は親切でかしこいから

カンマやセミコロンなどがある箇所で切る

，（カンマ）は日本語の読点と似ていて，やはり一拍おいて読む箇所を示しています。当然カンマのある箇所では切って読んでいきます。―（ダッシュ）や；（セミコロン）などのマークの箇所でも切って読んでいきます。

He was born / in Beijing, / the big city in China.
主文　前置詞＋名詞＋カンマ　同格説明
彼は生まれた / 北京で / 中国の大都市の

⇒別冊 p.5

解答と解説

解答

(1) ①　(2) ①

解説

(1) 第 1・2 文の内容から考えて，**1** が正解。

選択肢の和訳

(1) この案内は何のためのものか。

○ 1 図書館で仕事の手伝いをする人を見つけるため。
× 2 子供たちに本を売るため。
× 3 人々に新しい図書館について伝えるため。
× 4 子守をする人々を見つけるため。

(2) 読み方の練習を行うのは Reading club であることが第 3 文からわかり，またそれに続く第 4 文の後の（　）内の記述から，開催（かいさい）日時が土曜日と日曜日の午後 1 時～午後 4 時だとわかる。したがって，**1** が正解。

選択肢の和訳

(2) 子供たちが読む練習をするのを手助けできるのはいつか。

○ 1 毎週末の午後 1 時から午後 4 時の間。
× 2 毎週土曜日の午前 10 時 30 分から午前 11 時 30 分の間。
× 3 毎週日曜日の午前 10 時 30 分から午前 11 時 30 分の間。
× 4 平日の午後 5 時から午後 6 時の間。

語句

DOWN LOAD

〈タイトル〉

☐ Volunteers Wanted　ボランティア募集（ぼしゅう）

〈本文〉

☐ practice	(動) ～を練習する
☐ story time	お話（読み聞かせ）の時間
☐ kid	(名) 子供

〈設問・選択肢〉

☐ notice	(名) 通知，案内，掲示（けいじ）
☐ babysit	(動) ～の子守をする

構造確認 ※誤読した部分の確認に使用してください。

⇒別冊 p.5

① We need people 〈who love [reading] and [spending time (with children)]〉.

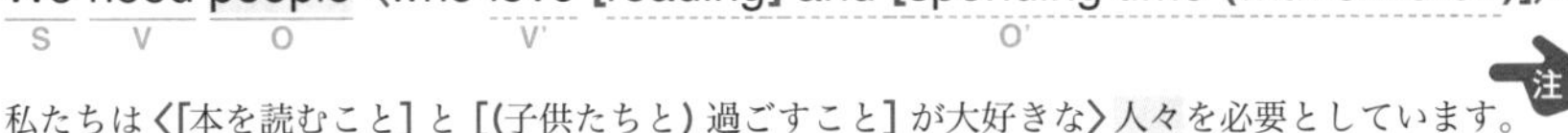

私たちは〈[本を読むこと] と [(子供たちと) 過ごすこと] が大好きな〉人々を必要としています。

② There are many ways 〈to help (at the library)〉:

注2

〈(図書館で) (仕事を) 手伝う〉方法はたくさんあります：

③ Reading club — Children 〈from 5 to 13 years old〉 come (to the library) (to practice reading).

読書クラブ —〈5 歳から 13 歳の〉子供たちが (読み方を練習するために) (図書館に) 来ます。

④ We need volunteers 〈to help them〉. (Saturdays and Sundays from 1:00 p.m. to 4:00 p.m.)

注3

私たちは〈彼ら (その子供たち) の手助けをする〉ボランティアが必要です。(毎週土曜日と日曜日の午後 1 時から午後 4 時まで)

⑤ Book readers — We have story time (on Saturday mornings).

本の朗読者 — (毎週土曜日の午前中に) お話 (読み聞かせ) の時間があります。

⑥ Read a book (to children 〈under 6 years old〉). (Saturdays from 10:30 a.m. to 11:30 a.m.)

(〈6 歳未満の〉子供たちに) 本を読み聞かせてください。(毎週土曜日の午前 10 時 30 分から午前 11 時 30 分まで)

⑦ Computer teachers — Teach kids to use computers. (Mondays and Wednesdays from 5:00 p.m. to 6:00 p.m.) 

V O

コンピュータの指導者 — 子供たちにコンピュータの使い方を教えてください。(毎週月曜日と水曜日の午後5時から午後6時まで)

注1 この文での who は関係代名詞で，love の主語の働きをしています。直前の people という名詞を後ろで説明するために使われています。

注2 この文での to 不定詞は形容詞のような働きをしていて，「…する」という意味で直前の ways という名詞を修飾しています。

注3 この文での to 不定詞は形容詞のような働きをしていて，「…するための」という意味で直前の volunteers という名詞を修飾しています。

注4 動詞の原形で始まる命令文で「…してください」という意味になります。

注5 teach 人 to V は「人に V すること（V のしかた）を教える」という意味になります。

サイトトランスレーション

⇒別冊 p.5

We need /	私たちは必要としています
people /	人々を
who love /	大好きである
reading and spending time /	本を読むことと時間を過ごすことが
with children. //	子供たちと。
There are many ways /	たくさんの方法があります
to help /	仕事を手伝うための
at the library: //	図書館で：
Reading club — /	読書クラブ—
Children /	子供たちが
from 5 to 13 years old /	5 歳から 13 歳の
come to the library /	図書館に来ます
to practice reading. //	読み方を練習するために。
We need /	私たちは必要です
volunteers /	ボランティアが
to help them. //	その子供たちの手助けをするための。
(Saturdays and Sundays /	（毎週土曜日と日曜日
from 1:00 p.m. to 4:00 p.m.) //	午後 1 時から午後 4 時まで）
Book readers — /	本の朗読者—
We have story time /	お話（読み聞かせ）の時間があります
on Saturday mornings. //	毎週土曜日の午前中に。

Read a book /	本を読んでください
to children /	子供たちに
under 6 years old. //	6 歳未満の。
(Saturdays /	（毎週土曜日の
from 10:30 a.m. to 11:30 a.m.) //	午前 10 時 30 分から午前 11 時 30 分まで）
Computer teachers — /	コンピュータの指導者―
Teach kids /	子供たちに教えてください
to use computers. //	コンピュータの使い方を。
(Mondays and Wednesdays /	（毎週月曜日と水曜日
from 5:00 p.m. to 6:00 p.m.) //	午後 5 時から午後 6 時まで）

問題英文と全訳

⇒別冊 p.5

Volunteers Wanted at Ferndale Library!

We need people who love reading and spending time with children. There are many ways to help at the library:

Reading club—Children from 5 to 13 years old come to the library to practice reading. We need volunteers to help them. (Saturdays and Sundays from 1:00 p.m. to 4:00 p.m.)

Book readers—We have story time on Saturday mornings. Read a book to children under 6 years old. (Saturdays from 10:30 a.m. to 11:30 a.m.)

Computer teachers—Teach kids to use computers. (Mondays and Wednesdays from 5:00 p.m. to 6:00 p.m.)

ファーンデール図書館のボランティア募集！

私たちは，本を読むことと子供たちと過ごすことが大好きな人々を必要としています。図書館で仕事を手伝う方法はたくさんあります：

読書クラブ—5歳から13歳の子供たちが，読み方を練習するために図書館に来ます。その子供たちの手助けをするボランティアが必要です。（毎週土曜日と日曜日の午後1時から午後4時まで）

本の朗読者—毎週土曜日の午前中に，読み聞かせの時間があります。6歳未満の子供たちに本を読み聞かせてください。（毎週土曜日の午前10時30分から午前11時30分まで）

コンピュータの指導者—子供たちにコンピュータの使い方を教えてください。（毎週月曜日と水曜日午後5時から午後6時まで）

⇒別冊 p.6

解答と解説

解答

(1) ③　(2) ④

解説

(1) リチャード・ウィルソンに関しては，第2文のOur guide, Richard Wilson, teaches you many interesting things about the trees and flowers. から，木や花について教えてくれる公園のガイドだとわかる。また，第6文のOur walks start every Sunday at 10:00 a.m. から，毎週日曜日の午前10時に園内散歩が行われていることがわかる。以上から考えて，**3**が正解。

選択肢の和訳

(1) 毎週日曜日の午前10時に，人々はリチャード・ウィルソンと何ができるか。

× 1 花を植える。
× 2 野球をする。
○ 3 自然について学ぶ。
× 4 公園を清掃(せいそう)する。

(2) 第7文にWe leave from the east baseball field.（私たちは東部野球場から出発します。）とある。その前の第6文から，Weは園内散歩に参加する（ために集合した）人々のことだとわかるから，**4**が正解。

選択肢の和訳

(2) 人々はどこに集まるか。

× 1 コリングウッド駅。
× 2 グレンウッドタウン。
× 3 観光案内所。
○ 4 東部野球場。

語句

DOWNLOAD

〈本文〉

□ have fun ～ing	～して楽しむ
□ guide	(名) ガイド，案内人
□ lavender	(名) ラベンダー
□ deer	(名) シカ
□ visitor center	ビジターセンター，案内所

〈設問・選択肢〉

□ plant	(動) ～を植える
□ nature	(名) 自然
□ clean up ～	～を清掃する
□ meet	(動) (人が) 集まる

構造確認 ※誤読した部分の確認に使用してください。

⇒別冊 p.6

① Have fun seeing the beautiful plants (in Collingwood Park). 

V O

(コリングウッド公園で) 美しい植物を見て楽しんでください。

② Our guide, Richard Wilson, teaches you many interesting things 〈about the trees and flowers〉.

S V O O

当公園の案内人であるリチャード・ウィルソンが〈木や花について〉多くの興味深いことをあなたにお教えします。

③ (This month), the lavenders are beautiful.

(今月は), ラベンダーがきれいです。

④ (If you're lucky), you may (also) see a deer! 

S' V' C' S V O

(運がよければ), シカ (も) 見られるかもしれません！

⑤ Bring your camera.

カメラを持ってきてください。

⑥ Our walks start (every Sunday) (at 10:00 a.m.)

S V

当公園の (園内) 散歩は (毎週日曜日の) (午前 10 時に) 始まります。

⑦ We leave (from the east baseball field).

私たちは (東部野球場から) 出発します。

⑧ The walk ends (at the visitor center) (at 11:30 a.m.)
S V

散歩は（午前11時30分に）（観光案内所で）終わります。

⑨ (To get to the park), take the Green Line 〈to Collingwood Station〉 or 

Bus #17 〈to the Glenwood Town〉.
V O① O②

（公園へ来るには），〈コリングウッド駅行きの〉グリーン線，または〈グレンウッドタウン行きの〉17番バスに乗ってください。

⑩ Call 555-4267 (for more information).
V O

（詳しくは）555-4267へお電話ください。

注1 動詞の原形で始まる命令文で「…してください」という意味になります。have fun Ving は「Vすることを楽しむ」という意味です。

注2 if という接続詞（つなぎ言葉）の後ろには主語と動詞が続き，if S V という形で「S が V するならば」という意味になります。

注3 この文での to 不定詞は副詞のような働きをしていて「…するためには」という意味で，目的を表すために使われています。

Unit 2

サイトトランスレーション

⇒別冊 p.6

Have fun /	楽しんでください
seeing the beautiful plants /	美しい植物を見て
in Collingwood Park. //	コリングウッド公園で。
Our guide, /	当公園の案内人,
Richard Wilson, /	リチャード・ウィルソンが,
teaches you /	あなたにお教えします
many interesting things /	多くの興味深いことを
about trees and flowers. //	木や花についての。
This month, /	今月は,
the lavenders are beautiful. //	ラベンダーがきれいです。
If you're lucky, /	あなたが運がよければ,
you may also see /	また，見られるかもしれません
a deer! //	シカを！
Bring /	持ってきてください
your camera. //	カメラを。
Our walks start /	園内散歩は始まります
every Sunday /	毎週日曜日
at 10:00 a.m. //	午前 10 時に。
We leave /	私たちは出発します
from the east baseball field. //	東部野球場から。
The walk ends /	散歩は終わります

at the visitor center /	観光案内所で
at 11:30 a.m. //	午前 11 時 30 分に。
To get to the park, /	公園へ着くには,
take the Green Line /	グリーン線に乗ってください
to Collingwood Station /	コリングウッド駅行きの
or /	または
Bus #17 /	17 番バスに
to the Glenwood Town. //	グレンウッドタウン行きの。
Call 555-4267 /	555-4267 へ電話してください
for more information. //	詳しくは。

問題英文と全訳

⇒別冊 p.6

Collingwood Park

Have fun seeing the beautiful plants in Collingwood Park. Our guide, Richard Wilson, teaches you many interesting things about the trees and flowers. This month, the lavenders are beautiful. If you're lucky, you may also see a deer! Bring your camera.

Our walks start every Sunday at 10:00 a.m. We leave from the east baseball field. The walk ends at the visitor center at 11:30 a.m. To get to the park, take the Green Line to Collingwood Station or Bus #17 to the Glenwood Town.

Call 555-4267 for more information.

コリングウッド公園

コリングウッド公園で美しい植物を見て楽しんでください。当公園の案内人であるリチャード・ウィルソンが，木や花について多くの興味深いことをあなたにお教えします。今月はラベンダーがきれいです。運がよければ，シカも見られるかもしれません！　カメラをご持参ください。

園内散歩は毎週日曜日の午前10時に始まります。私たちは東部野球場から出発します。散歩は午前11時30分に，観光案内所で終わります。公園へは，コリングウッド駅行きのグリーン線，またはグレンウッドタウン行きの17番バスに乗ってください。

詳しくは，555-4267へお電話ください。

⇒別冊 p.7

解答と解説

解答

(1) ②　(2) ①

解説

(1) 第 1 文の We can teach you how to make a robot yourself.(私たちは自分でロボットを作る方法を教えます。) から考えて，**2** が正解。

選択肢の和訳

(1) この案内は…ことを望む人々のためのものである

× 1 ロボット製作コンテストを見る。

○ 2 自分のロボットを作る。

× 3 ロボットのレースを見る。

× 4 おもちゃのロボットを買う。

(2) 第 4 文(最後から 2 つめの文)On Saturday, June 2 at 10:00 a.m., you can take a special class to try making robots. から，6 月 2 日に特別なクラスが受けられることがわかり，それに続く最後の文に It's free!(それは無料です！)とある。したがって，**1** が正解。

選択肢の和訳

(2) 無料の授業はいつ受けられるか。

○ 1 6月2日に。

× 2 6月4日に。

× 3 6月5日に。

× 4 7月25日に。

語句

〈タイトル〉

- □ robot　(名) ロボット

〈本文〉

- □ racing < race　(動) レース［競走］をする
- □ pick ～ up　～を拾う
- □ climb　(動) 登る
- □ beginner　(名) 初心者
- □ cost　(名) 費用
- □ advanced　(形) 上級の
- □ take a class　授業を受ける
- □ special　(形) 特別の
- □ try ～ing　試しに～してみる
- □ free　(形) 無料の

〈設問・選択肢〉

- □ notice　(名) 通知，案内，掲示
- □ robot-building contest　ロボット製作コンテスト
- □ own　(形) 自分自身の

構造確認 ※誤読した部分の確認に使用してください。

⇒別冊 p.7

① We can teach you [how to make a robot (yourself)]. 

S V O O

私たちは [(自分で) ロボットを作る方法] を教えます。

② (After you make it), you can play (with your robot)! 

S' V' O' S V

(それを作った後は), (自分のロボットで) 遊ぶことができます！

③ You can make robots 〈for [racing], [picking things up], and [climbing]〉.

S V O

〈[レースをしたり], [物を拾ったり], [クライミングをしたりする] ための〉ロボットを作ることができます。

Class A: Beginner class (Monday and Wednesday from 5:00 p.m. to 6:00 p.m., June 4 - July 25. Cost: $250)

クラスA：初心者クラス (6月4日～7月25日, 月曜日と水曜日の午後5時から午後6時まで。費用は250ドル)

Class B: Advanced class (Tuesday and Friday from 5:00 p.m. to 6:30 p.m., June 5 - July 27. Cost: $300)

クラスB：上級者クラス (6月5日～7月27日, 火曜日と金曜日の午後5時から午後6時30分まで。費用は300ドル)

④ (On Saturday), (June 2 at 10:00 a.m.), you can take a special class 〈to try [making robots]〉. 注3

S V O

(6月2日 (土曜日の,) 午前10時に) 〈[ロボット作り] を試してみる〉特別クラスを受講できます。

⑤ It's free!

S V C

それは無料です！

注1 how to V は「どのようにして V するか」という意味で，名詞の働きをするカタマリを作ります。

注2 この文での after は接続詞として使われています。after S V で「S が V する後で」という意味になります。

注3 この文での to 不定詞は形容詞のような働きをしていて，直前の a special class という名詞を修飾しています。

Unit 3

サイトトランスレーション

⇒別冊 p.7

We can teach you /	私たちは教えることができます
how to make a robot yourself. //	自分でロボットを作る方法を。
After you make it, /	それを作った後は,
you can play /	遊ぶことができます
with your robot! //	自分のロボットで！
You can make robots /	ロボットを作ることができます
for racing, picking things up, and climbing. //	レースをしたり，物を拾ったり，クライミングをしたりするための。
Class A: /	クラスＡ：
Beginner class /	初心者クラス
(Monday and Wednesday /	（月曜日と水曜日
from 5:00 p.m. to 6:00 p.m., /	午後５時から午後６時まで,
June 4 - July 25. //	６月４日～７月25日。
Cost: $250) //	費用：250ドル）
Class B: /	クラスＢ：
Advanced class /	上級者クラス
(Tuesday and Friday /	（火曜日と金曜日
from 5:00 p.m. to 6:30 p.m., /	午後５時から午後６時30分まで,
June 5 - July 27. //	６月５日～７月27日。
Cost: $300) //	費用：300ドル）
On Saturday, /	土曜日,
June 2 /	６月２日

at 10:00 a.m., /	午前 10 時に,
you can take /	受講できます
a special class /	特別クラスを
to try making robots. //	ロボット作りを試してみるための。
It's free! //	それは無料です！
Supertech Robot School /	スーパーテックロボット教室
23 Windemere Lane /	ウィンダミア通り 23
Telephone: 555-2452 //	電話：555-2452

問題英文と全訳

⇒別冊 p.7

Do you like robots?

We can teach you how to make a robot yourself. After you make it, you can play with your robot! You can make robots for racing, picking things up, and climbing.

Class A: Beginner class (Monday and Wednesday from 5:00 p.m. to 6:00 p.m., June 4 – July 25. Cost: $250)
Class B: Advanced class (Tuesday and Friday from 5:00 p.m. to 6:30 p.m., June 5 – July 27. Cost: $300)

On Saturday, June 2 at 10:00 a.m., you can take a special class to try making robots. It's free!

Supertech Robot School
23 Windemere Lane
Telephone: 555-2452

ロボットは好きですか？

私たちは，自分でロボットを作る方法を教えます。作った後は，自分のロボットで遊ぶことができます！　レースをしたり，物を拾ったり，クライミングをしたりするためのロボットを作ることができます。

クラスA：初心者クラス(6月4日～7月25日，月曜日と水曜日の午後5時から午後6時まで。費用は250ドル)

クラスB：上級者クラス(6月5日～7月27日，火曜日と金曜日の午後5時から午後6時30分まで。費用は300ドル)

6月2日土曜日の午前10時に，ロボット作りを試してみる特別クラスを受講できます。無料です！

スーパーテックロボット教室
ウィンダミア通り23
電話：555-2452

Unit 4

⇒別冊 p.8

解答と解説

解答

(1) ①　(2) ③

解説

(1) 第1文に有名作家のトッド・バーネット氏が来校すること，第2文に彼が30の異なる国々を訪ねていること，そして第3文に彼が今までに訪れた興味深い場所のいくつかについて話す予定であることが述べられている。したがって，**1** が正解。

選択肢の和訳

(1) 9月21日に何が起こるか。

○1 ある作家がさまざまな国について話す。

×2 他の国の生徒たちが訪れる。

×3 本の販売がある。

×4 クラスの写真が撮られる。

---

(2) 最後の文に There will be only 40 seats (40席しかない) とあるので，**3** が正解。

選択肢の和訳

(2) 何人がその催しに行けるか。

×1 20人。

×2 30人。

○3 40人。

×4 50人。

語句

DOWNLOAD

〈本文〉

□ more than ～	～より多くの
□ bestseller	(名) ベストセラー
□ whiteboard	(名) ホワイトボード
□ outside	(前) ～の外に
□ school office	職員室
□ quickly	(副) 急いで，すばやく

〈設問・選択肢〉

□ event	(名) 催し，行事

Unit 4

構造確認

※誤読した部分の確認に使用してください。

⇒別冊 p.8

① The famous writer Todd Burnett is coming (to Northview High School). 

有名作家のトッド・バーネット氏が (ノースビュー高校に) 来ます。

② He has visited 30 different countries, and he writes (about the places 〈he visited〉) (in his books). 注2

彼は 30 の異なる国々を訪ね，(自著の中で) (〈訪問した〉場所について) 書いています。

③ He is going to talk (about some 〈of the interesting places 〈that he has visited〉〉). 注3

彼は (〈〈訪問した〉興味深い場所の〉いくつかについて) 話す予定です。

④ He will (also) show 50 photos 〈of his favorite places〉.

彼は (また) 〈お気に入りの場所の〉50 枚の写真も見せてくれるでしょう。

⑤ Mr. Burnett has written more than 20 books, and many 〈of them〉 are bestsellers. 

バーネット氏は 20 冊を超える本を書いており，〈それらの〉多くはベストセラーです。

Where: The school library

場所：校内図書館

When: September 21 at 3:30 p.m.

日時：9 月 21 日 午後 3 時 30 分

⑥ You can sign up (by [writing your name on the whiteboard 〈outside the school office〉]).

([〈職員室の外の〉ホワイトボードに名前を書くこと] で) 申し込めます。

⑦ There will be (only) 40 seats, so sign up (quickly)!

40 席 (のみ) なので，(すぐに) 申し込んでください！

注1　この文のように，現在進行形は未来の予定を表すために使われることもあります。

注2　have[has] ＋過去分詞 は現在完了形で，この文では，これまでの主語の経験を表すために使われています。このように，現在完了形は過去からつながる現状を表すために使われます。

注3　that は関係代名詞です。that 以下の内容は，直前の the interesting places という名詞を修飾しています。

注4　more than ～は「～よりも多く」という意味です。more は many の比較級です。

サイトトランスレーション

⇒別冊 p.8

The famous writer /	有名作家の
Todd Burnett /	トッド・バーネット氏が
is coming /	来ます
to Northview High School. //	ノースビュー高校に。
He has visited /	彼は訪ねてきました
30 different countries, /	30 の異なる国々を，
and he writes /	そして彼は書いています
about the places /	場所について
he visited /	彼が訪問した
in his books. //	自著の中で。
He is going to talk /	彼は話す予定です
about some of the interesting places /	興味深い場所のいくつかについて
that he has visited. //	彼が訪問したことのある。
He will also show /	彼はまた見せるでしょう
50 photos /	50 枚の写真を
of his favorite places. //	お気に入りの場所の。
Mr. Burnett has written /	バーネット氏は書いています
more than 20 books, /	20 冊を超える本を，
and many of them /	そしてそれらの多くは
are bestsellers. //	ベストセラーです。
Where: /	場所：

The school library //	校内図書館
When: /	日時：
September 21 /	9月21日
at 3:30 p.m. //	午後3時30分
You can sign up /	申し込めます
by writing your name /	名前を書くことで
on the whiteboard /	ホワイトボードに
outside the school office. //	職員室の外の。
There will be only 40 seats, /	40席しかありません，
so sign up quickly! //	なのですぐに申し込んでください！

問題英文と全訳

⇒別冊 p.8

To All Students

The famous writer Todd Burnett is coming to Northview High School. He has visited 30 different countries, and he writes about the places he visited in his books. He is going to talk about some of the interesting places that he has visited. He will also show 50 photos of his favorite places. Mr. Burnett has written more than 20 books, and many of them are bestsellers.

Where: The school library
When: September 21 at 3:30 p.m.

You can sign up by writing your name on the whiteboard outside the school office. There will be only 40 seats, so sign up quickly!

全校生徒へ

有名作家のトッド・バーネット氏が，ノースビュー高校にいらっしゃいます。彼は30の異なる国々を訪ね，自著の中で訪問した場所について書いています。彼は，訪問した興味深い場所のいくつかについて話す予定です。また，お気に入りの場所の50枚の写真も見せてくれるでしょう。バーネット氏は20冊以上の本を書き，それらの多くはベストセラーです。

場所：校内図書館
日時：9月21日 午後3時30分

職員室の外のホワイトボードに名前を書くことで申し込めます。40席しかないので，すぐに申し込んでください！

Unit 5

⇒別冊 p.9

解答と解説

解答

(1) ④　(2) ③

解説

(1) 第 4 文に We need 15 performers for the show.(演芸会には 15 人の出場者が必要です。) とあるので，**4** が正解。

選択肢の和訳

(1) 演芸会に参加するのは何人か。

×1 2 人。

×2 8 人。

×3 12 人。

○4 15 人。

---

(2) 第 5 文に First prize will be a free dinner(1 等賞は無料の夕食です) とあるので，**3** が正解。

選択肢の和訳

(2) 最も優れた演技をした人は…を受けられる

×1 商品券。

×2 T シャツ。

○3 無料の食事。

×4 ダンスの授業。

語句

DOWN LOAD

〈本文〉

- □ invite　(動) ～を誘(さそ)う
- □ take part in ～　～に参加する
- □ talent show　演芸 (発表) 会
- □ do magic　手品をする
- □ performance　(名) 演技
- □ performer　(名) 演技者，出演者
- □ prize　(名) 賞
- □ gift coupon　商品券
- □ volunteer　(名) ボランティア
- □ clean up　清掃する
- □ would like to *do*　～したい
- □ sign up　申し込む

構造確認 ※誤読した部分の確認に使用してください。

⇒別冊 p.9

① Redford Senior High School is inviting people 〈who can take part (in this year's talent show) (on November 12)〉.
S V O V'

レッドフォード高校は〈(11 月 12 日にある) (今年の演芸会に) 参加できる〉人を求めています。

② (If you can sing, play music, dance, or do magic), you can be (in the show).
S' V'① V'② O'② V'③ V'④ O'④ S V

注1

(歌ったり，音楽を演奏したり，踊ったり，手品をしたりすることができれば)，(演芸会に) 参加できます。

③ Your performance must be between 2 and 8 minutes long.
S V C

演技 (の時間) は 2 ～ 8 分の長さと決められています。

④ We need 15 performers (for the show).
S V O

(演芸会には) 15 人の出場者が必要です。

⑤ First prize will be a free dinner 〈at Rocky's Hamburgers〉.
S V C

1 等賞は〈ロッキーズ・ハンバーガーズでの〉無料の夕食です。

⑥ Second prize will be a $30 gift coupon 〈from Pressler Books〉.
S V C

2 等賞は〈プレスラ・ブックスの〉30 ドルの商品券です。

⑦ Third prize will be a T-shirt 〈from Collier Fashions〉.
S V C

3 等賞は〈コリアー・ファッションズの〉T シャツです。

⑧ We (also) need 8 volunteers 〈to sell tickets and clean up (after the show)〉.
S V O
注2

我々は(また)〈チケット販売〉と〈(演芸会終了後の)清掃を行う〉8名のボランティアも求めています。

⑨ (If you would like to be (in the talent show)), sign up (in Ms. Cameron's
S' V' V
homeroom) (by 4:00 p.m. on October 30).
注3

((演芸会に)参加したい方は),(10月30日の午後4時までに)(キャメロン先生のホームルームで)申し込んでください。

注1 if は接続詞で, if S V という形で「もしも S が V するならば」という意味のカタマリを作ります。

注2 to 不定詞は形容詞のような働きをし, 直前の名詞を修飾することができます。この文での to sell ... の部分は, 8 volunteers という名詞を修飾しています。

注3 by という前置詞は「～までに」という意味で, 期限を表す場合に使います。

サイトトランスレーション

⇒別冊 p.9

Redford Senior High School is inviting /	レッドフォード高校は求めています
people who can take part /	参加できる人を
in this year's talent show /	今年の演芸会に
on November 12. //	11 月 12 日の。
If you can sing, /	歌ったりすることができるならば,
play music, /	音楽を演奏したり,
dance, /	踊ったり,
or do magic, /	手品をしたり,
you can be /	参加できます
in the show. //	演芸会に。
Your performance /	演技は
must be between 2 and 8 minutes long. //	2～8 分の長さでなくてはなりません。
We need /	私たちは必要です
15 performers /	15 人の出場者が
for the show. //	演芸会には。
First prize /	1 等賞は
will be a free dinner /	無料の夕食です
at Rocky's Hamburgers. //	ロッキーズ・ハンバーガーズでの。
Second prize /	2 等賞は
will be a $30 gift coupon /	30 ドルの商品券です
from Pressler Books. //	プレスラ・ブックスの。

Third prize /	3等賞は
will be a T-shirt /	Tシャツです
from Collier Fashions. //	コリアー・ファッションズの。
We also need /	私たちはまた求めています
8 volunteers /	8名のボランティアを
to sell tickets /	チケットを販売する
and clean up /	そして清掃を行う
after the show. //	演芸会終了後に。
If you would like to be /	もし参加を希望するなら
in the talent show, /	演芸会への,
sign up /	申し込んでください
in Ms. Cameron's homeroom /	キャメロン先生のホームルームで
by 4:00 p.m. /	午後4時までに
on October 30. //	10月30日の。

問題英文と全訳

⇒別冊 p.9

Show Us Your Talent!

Redford Senior High School is inviting people who can take part in this year's talent show on November 12.
If you can sing, play music, dance, or do magic, you can be in the show. Your performance must be between 2 and 8 minutes long. We need 15 performers for the show.
First prize will be a free dinner at Rocky's Hamburgers. Second prize will be a $30 gift coupon from Pressler Books. Third prize will be a T-shirt from Collier Fashions.
We also need 8 volunteers to sell tickets and clean up after the show.
If you would like to be in the talent show, sign up in Ms. Cameron's homeroom by 4:00 p.m. on October 30.

あなたの才能を私たちに見せてください！

レッドフォード高校では，11 月 12 日に行われる今年の演芸会に参加できる人を求めています。歌ったり，音楽を演奏したり，踊ったり，手品をしたりすることができれば，演芸会に参加できます。演技の時間は 2 ～ 8 分の長さと決められています。演芸会には 15 人の出場者が必要です。
1 等賞は，ロッキーズ・ハンバーガーズでの無料の夕食です。2 等賞は，プレスラ・ブックスの 30 ドルの商品券です。3 等賞は，コリアー・ファッションズの T シャツです。
我々はまた，チケット販売と演芸会終了後の清掃を行うボランティアも 8 名求めています。
演芸会に参加したい方は，10 月 30 日の午後 4 時までにキャメロン先生のホームルームで申し込んでください。

Unit 6

⇒別冊 p.10 ~ 11

解答と解説

解答

(1) ②　(2) ①　(3) ①

解説

(1) ブラッドリーのメール（1つめのメール）の第4・5文に I'll never forget driving the motorboat. No one ever let me do that before. とあるので，**2** が正解。

設問・選択肢の和訳

(1) ブラッドリーが初めてしたことは何だったか。

×1 おばの家に泊まった。　○2 モーターボートを運転した。

×3 泳ぎ方を学んだ。　×4 釣りに行った。

(2) ブラッドリーのメール（1つめのメール）の第10文に Mom says, "Thank you for the jam." とあるので，**1** が正解。

設問・選択肢の和訳

(2) ジェーンおばさんはブラッドリーの母親に何をあげたか。

○1 ジャム。　×2 写真。　×3 魚。　×4 ハンバーガー。

(3) ブラッドリーのメール（1つめのメール）の第8文の Please tell Uncle Martin again that I'm sorry about his fishing pole. と，ジェーンおばさんのメール（2つめのメール）の第2・3文の Don't worry about the fishing pole. Everybody drops things sometimes. から考えて，**1** が正解。

設問・選択肢の和訳

(3) ブラッドリーはなぜ申し訳ないと思っているのか。

○1 おじの釣りざおを壊した。　×2 コテージに長い間泊まりすぎた。

×3 モーターボートを壊した。　×4 ジャムを食べすぎた。

語句

DOWN LOAD

〈1つめのメール〉

□ thanks for ～ing	～してくれてありがとう
□ let O *do*	Oが～するのを許す
□ pool	(名) プール
□ twice as far	2倍遠くへ
□ motorboat	(名) モーターボート
□ pole	(名) さお，棒
□ careful	(形) 注意深い，慎重な
□ pick	(動) ～を摘む
□ strawberry	(名) イチゴ
□ blueberry	(名) ブルーベリー
□ stay with ～	～の家に泊まる

〈2つめのメール〉

□ worry about ～	～のことを心配する
□ sometimes	(副) 時々，時には
□ fix	(動) ～を修理する
□ work fine	正しく作動する
□ cottage	(名) (いなかの小さな) 家

〈設問・選択肢〉

□ for the first time	初めて

構造確認 ※誤読した部分の確認に使用してください。

⇒別冊 p.10 ～ 11

1つめのメール ブラッドリー・ホーキンスからジェーン・ウィルソンへ／件名：ありがとう！

①Thanks so much (for [letting me stay at your house (again) (this summer)]). 注1

([(今年の夏) (再び) 僕を家に泊まらせてくれ] て) どうもありがとう。

②It's (really) beautiful (at Lake Deerfield), and it was fun [to go swimming (with you and Uncle Martin) (every morning)].

S① V① C① S② V② C②

(ディアフィールド湖は) (本当に) きれいで，[(毎日午前中に) (おばさんとマーティンおじさんと一緒に) 泳ぎに行ったこと] が楽しかったです。

③(After we got (home)), Mom took me (to the pool), and she was surprised (because I can swim (twice as far now)).

S'① V'① S① V① O① S② V② C② S'② V'②

((家に) 帰ったあと)，母は僕を (プールに) 連れて行って，(僕が (今では2倍の距離) 泳ぐことができるので) 驚いていました。

④I'll (never) forget [driving the motorboat].

S V O

[モーターボートを運転したこと] を僕は (決して) 忘れ (ない) でしょう。

⑤No one (ever) let me do that (before).

S V O

(以前に) 誰も僕にそれをさせたことがありませんでした。

⑥I enjoyed [going really fast (all around the lake)].

S V O

[(湖じゅうを) とても速く走るの] を楽しみました。

⑦It was exciting.

S V C

わくわくしました。

⑧ Please tell Uncle Martin (again) [that I'm sorry (about his fishing pole)].
V O O S' V' C'

マーティンおじさんに（もう一度）[（おじさんの釣りざおについて）申し訳なく思っている] と伝えてください。

⑨ I was not careful (with it).
S V C

僕は（それ（釣りざお）に）注意していませんでした。

⑩ Mom says, "Thank you (for the jam)."
S V

母は「（ジャムを）ありがとう」と言っています。

⑪ It was fun [picking strawberries and blueberries].
S V C

[イチゴとブルーベリーを摘むの] は楽しかったです。

⑫ You make the best jam 〈I've (ever) eaten〉!
S V O S' V'

おばさんは〈僕が（これまでに）食べた中で〉最高のジャムを作ります！

⑬ I hope [I can stay (with you) (again) (next year)].
S V O S' V'

[（来年）（また）（おばさんのところに）泊まれる] といいなと思います。

ジェーン・ウィルソンからブラッドリー・ホーキンスへ／件名：来てくれてありがとう

① We're glad you had a good time (with us).
S V C S' V' O'

あなたが（私たちと）楽しい時間を過ごせてうれしいです。

② Don't worry (about the fishing pole).
V

（釣りざおについては）心配しないで。

③ Everybody drops things (sometimes).
S V O

誰でも（時々）物を落とします。

④ Uncle Martin fixed it (yesterday), and it works (fine) (now).
S① V① O① S② V②

(昨日) マーティンおじさんがそれを直したので，(今では) (ちゃんと) 使えます。

⑤ He caught three fish (this morning).
S V O

(今朝) おじさんは魚を３匹釣りました。

⑥ We took lots of pictures 〈of you〉 (at the cottage), so we're going to send them (to you) (soon).
S① V① O① S② V② O②

(コテージで) 〈あなたの〉写真をたくさん撮ったので，それらを (あなたに) (すぐに) 送ります。

⑦ I think [you'll like the picture 〈of [you and the hamburgers]〉].
S V OS' V' O'

[あなたは〈[自分とハンバーガー] の〉写真を気に入る] と思います。

⑧ We were surprised that you could eat five 〈of them〉.
S V C S' V' O'

あなたが〈それらを〉5 つ食べられることに私たちは驚きました。

⑨ We hope [that you'll be able to stay (with us) (again) (next summer)].
S V O S' V'

[あなたが (また) (来年の夏も) (私たちのところに) 泊まれる] といいなと思います。

注1 let 人 V は「人に V するのを許す」という意味です。動詞の前に to が入らないことに注意しましょう。

注2 it は仮主語で，to go ... という不定詞の部分を指しています。「それ」という意味にはならないので注意しましょう。

注3 forget Ving は「V したことを忘れる」という意味で，Ving の部分は動名詞です。

注4 it は仮主語で，picking ... の部分を指しています。このように，仮主語が動名詞を指すのは珍しい形なので，参考程度に見ておけば大丈夫です。

注5 the 最上級 that S have[has] ever 過去分詞 は「S がこれまでに V した中でいちばん…な～」という意味の構文です。

注6 be glad (that) S V は「S が V してうれしい」という意味の，会話やメールなどでよく使う表現です。

Unit 6

サイトトランスレーション

⇒別冊 p.10 ~ 11

1 Hi Aunt Jane, /	こんにちは，ジェーンおばさん，
Thanks so much /	どうもありがとう
for letting me stay /	泊まらせてくれて
at your house /	おばさんの家に
again this summer. //	再び今年の夏。
It's really beautiful /	本当にきれいです
at Lake Deerfield, /	ディアフィールド湖は，
and it was fun /	楽しかったです
to go swimming /	泳ぎに行くことは
with you and Uncle Martin /	おばさんとマーティンおじさんと一緒に
every morning. //	毎日午前中に。
After we got home, /	家に帰ったあと，
Mom took me /	母が僕を連れて行ってくれました
to the pool, /	プールに，
and she was surprised /	彼女は驚いていました
because I can swim /	僕が泳ぐことができるので
twice as far /	２倍の距離
now. //	今では。
I'll never forget /	僕は決して忘れません
driving the motorboat. //	モーターボートを運転したことを。
No one ever let me do that /	これまで誰も僕にそれをさせてくれませんでした

before. //	以前に。
I enjoyed /	僕は楽しみました
going really fast /	とても速く走るのを
all around the lake. //	湖じゅうを。
It was exciting. //	わくわくしました。
Please tell /	伝えてください
Uncle Martin again /	マーティンおじさんにもう一度
that I'm sorry /	僕が申し訳なく思っていると
about his fishing pole. //	おじさんの釣りざおのことを。
I was not careful /	僕は注意深くありませんでした
with it. //	それについて。
Mom says, /	母は言っています，
"Thank you /	「ありがとう
for the jam." //	ジャムを」と。
It was fun /	楽しかったです
picking strawberries and blueberries. //	イチゴとブルーベリーを摘むのは。
You make the best jam /	おばさんは最高のジャムを作ります
I've ever eaten! //	僕がこれまでに食べた中で！
I hope /	僕はいいなと思います
I can stay /	僕が泊まれたら
with you /	おばさんの家に
again next year. //	再び来年。
Love, /	じゃあまた，
Bradley //	ブラッドリー

2 Hi Bradley, /	こんにちは，ブラッドリー，
We’re glad /	私たちはうれしいです
you had a good time /	あなたが楽しく過ごせて
with us. //	私たちと。
Don’t worry /	心配しないで
about the fishing pole. //	釣りざおのことは。
Everybody drops /	誰でも落とします
things /	物を
sometimes. //	時々。
Uncle Martin fixed /	マーティンおじさんは直しました
it /	それを
yesterday, /	昨日，
and it works fine /	それはちゃんと使えます
now. //	今では。
He caught /	彼（マーティンおじさん）は釣りました
three fish /	3匹の魚を
this morning. //	今朝。
We took /	私たちは撮りました
lots of pictures /	たくさんの写真を
of you /	あなたの
at the cottage, /	コテージで，
so we’re going to send /	だから送ります
them /	それらを
to you soon. //	あなたにすぐに。

I think /	私は思います
you’ll like /	あなたは気に入ると
the picture of you /	自分の写真を
and the hamburgers. //	そしてハンバーガー（の）。
We were surprised /	私たちは驚きました
that you could eat /	あなたが食べられることに
five of them. //	それらを５つ。
We hope /	私たちはいいなと思います
that you’ll be able to stay /	あなたが泊まれると
with us /	私たちのところに
again next summer. //	再び来年の夏。
Love, /	愛をこめて，
Aunt Jane //	ジェーンおばさん

問題英文と全訳

⇒別冊 p.10 ~ 11

From: Bradley Hawkins
To: Jane Wilson
Date: August 28
Subject: Thanks!

Hi Aunt Jane,
Thanks so much for letting me stay at your house again this summer. It's really beautiful at Lake Deerfield, and it was fun to go swimming with you and Uncle Martin every morning. After we got home, Mom took me to the pool, and she was surprised because I can swim twice as far now. I'll never forget driving the motorboat. No one ever let me do that before. I enjoyed going really fast all around the lake. It was exciting. Please tell Uncle Martin again that I'm sorry about his fishing pole. I was not careful with it. Mom says, "Thank you for the jam." It was fun picking strawberries and blueberries. You make the best jam I've ever eaten! I hope I can stay with you again next year.
Love,
Bradley

From: Jane Wilson
To: Bradley Hawkins
Date: August 29
Subject: Thanks for coming

Hi Bradley,
We're glad you had a good time with us. Don't worry about the fishing pole. Everybody drops things sometimes. Uncle Martin fixed it yesterday, and it works fine now. He caught three fish this morning. We took lots of pictures of you at the cottage, so we're going to send them to you soon. I think you'll like the picture of you and the hamburgers. We were surprised that you could eat five of them. We hope that you'll be able to stay with us again next summer.
Love,
Aunt Jane

送信者：ブラッドリー・ホーキンス
受信者：ジェーン・ウィルソン
日付：8月28日
件名：ありがとう！

こんにちは，ジェーンおばさん
今年の夏もまた家に泊まらせてくれて，どうもありがとう。ディアフィールド湖は本当にきれいで，毎日午前中におばさんとマーティンおじさんと一緒に泳ぎに行って楽しかったです。家に帰ったあと，母が僕をプールに連れて行って，今では僕が２倍の距離を泳ぐことができるので驚いていました。モーターボートを運転したことは決して忘れません。それ以前に一度も運転させてもらったことがありませんでした。湖じゅうをとても速く走るのを楽しみました。わくわくしました。マーティンおじさんに，おじさんの釣りざおのことを申し訳なく思っているともう一度伝えてください。僕は釣りざおに注意していませんでした。母は「ジャムをありがとう」と言っています。イチゴとブルーベリーを摘むのは楽しかったです。おばさんは僕がこれまでに食べた中で最高のジャムを作ります！　来年また，おばさんの家に泊まれるとうれしいです。
じゃあまた，
ブラッドリー

送信者：ジェーン・ウィルソン
受信者：ブラッドリー・ホーキンス
日付：8月29日
件名：来てくれてありがとう

こんにちは，ブラッドリー
あなたが私たちと楽しく過ごせてうれしいです。釣りざおのことは心配しないで。誰でも時々物を落とします。昨日マーティンおじさんが直したので，今ではさおはちゃんと使えます。今朝おじさんは魚を３匹釣りました。コテージであなたの写真をたくさん撮ったので，すぐに送ります。あなたは自分とハンバーガーの写真を気に入ると思います。あなたが５つ食べられることに私たちは驚きました。来年の夏もまた，あなたがうちに泊まれるとうれしいです。
愛をこめて，
ジェーンおばさん

⇒別冊 p.12 ~ 13

解答と解説

解答

(1) ③　(2) ③　(3) ①

解説

(1) ウェンディの最初のメール(1つめのメール)の第2文の後半にI saw a video game, and I bought that とあるので，**3** が正解。

設問・選択肢の和訳

(1) ウェンディは祖母からのお金で何を買ったか。

×1 サッカーボール。　×2 腕時計。　○3 テレビゲーム。　×4 クラリネット。

---

(2) ウェンディの最初のメール (1 つめのメール) の第 6 文に after school, we have another practice for 90 minutes とあるので，**3** が正解。

設問・選択肢の和訳

(2) ウェンディは放課後どのくらい練習するか。

×1 30 分。　×2 1 時間。　○3 90 分。　×4 2 時間。

---

(3) ウェンディの 2 回めのメール(3 つめのメール)の第 6 文に She took a video とあり，この She は前文の Mom を指しているので，**1** が正解。

設問・選択肢の和訳

(3) ウェンディの母は何をしたか。

○1 コンサートの動画を撮影(さつえい)した。　×2 ウェンディに花をあげた。

×3 ウェンディの祖母のためにチケットを買った。　×4 友人をコンサートに招いた。

語句

DOWN LOAD

〈1 つめのメール〉

- □ plan to *do*　～することを計画する
- □ practice　(動) ～を練習する
- □ clarinet　(名) クラリネット

〈3 つめのメール〉

- □ a lot　たくさん
- □ performance　(名) 演奏
- □ be surprised to *do*　～して驚く
- □ borrow　(動) ～を借りる
- □ take a video　ビデオ［動画］を撮影する

〈設問・選択肢〉

- □ invite　(動) ～を招待する

構造確認 ※誤読した部分の確認に使用してください。

⇒別冊 p.12 ~ 13

1つめのメール ウェンディ・ピアスからバーバラ・ピアスへ／件名：ありがとう

① Thank you very much (for the birthday money).
V O

(誕生日祝いのお金を) ありがとうございます。

② I was planning to buy a new soccer ball or a watch, but I saw a video game, and I bought that.
S① V① O① S② V② O② S③ V③ O③

新しいサッカーボールか腕時計を買おうと計画していたけれど，テレビゲームが目に入って，それを買いました。

③ It's really fun, but Mom says [I can (only) play it (for 30 minutes every day)].
S①V① C① S② V② O② S' V' O'

それは本当に楽しいのですが，[私は (毎日 30 分) それで遊べる (だけ)] とママは言います。

④ I'm busy (because I have to practice the clarinet (for our school concert)).
S V C S' V' O'

私は ((校内コンサートのために) クラリネットを練習しなくてはならないので) 忙しいです。

⑤ We practice (for one hour) (in the morning).
S V

私たちは (朝) (1 時間) 練習します。

⑥ (Then) (after school), we have another practice (for 90 minutes).
S V O

(それから) (放課後に)，(90 分間の) 練習が他にあります。

⑦ Can you come (to the concert)?
V S

(コンサートに) 来ることはできますか。

⑧ It will be (on Saturday, October 2).
S V

それ（コンサート）は（10月2日，土曜日に）あります。

⑨ It will start (at 2:00 p.m.), and it will be about two hours long.
S① V① S② V② C②

それ（コンサート）は（午後2時に）始まって，約2時間の長さの予定です。

2つめのメール バーバラ・ピアスからウェンディ・ピアスへ／件名：コンサート

① I'm happy (to hear [you're enjoying the video game]). 
S V C S' V' O'

（[あなたがテレビゲームを楽しんでいる] と聞いて）うれしいです。

② It's great [that you're practicing the clarinet so much]. 
S V C S' V' O'

[クラリネットをそれほどたくさん練習しているの] はすばらしいことです。

③ I want to go (to your concert), but I will travel (to Weston) (that weekend).
S① V① S② V②

（あなたのコンサートに）行きたいけれど，私は（その週末に）（ウェストンへ）旅行するつもりです。

④ I'm going to visit a friend of mine 〈who lives (there)〉. 
S V O V'

〈（そこに）住んでいる〉友人を訪問する予定です。

⑤ I (already) bought tickets, so I can't change my plans.
S① V① O① S② V② O②

（もう）切符（きっぷ）を買ったので，計画を変更することができません。

⑥ I know [that you're a great clarinet player], so I'm sure the concert will be very good.
S① V① O① S'① V'① C'① S② V② C② S'② V'② C'②

[あなたがクラリネットがとても上手であること] は知っているので，きっとコンサートは大変すてきなものになるでしょう。

3つめのメール ウェンディ・ピアスからバーバラ・ピアスへ／件名：すべて終えました！

① I played (in the concert) (today)!
S V

(今日) (コンサートで) 演奏しました！

② I was nervous, but everybody clapped (a lot) (for our performance).
S① V① C① S② V②

緊張しましたが，みんな (私たちの演奏に) (たくさん) 拍手してくれました。

③ Thank you (for [sending the flowers]).
V O

([花を送ってくれ] て) ありがとう。

④ I was (really) surprised (to get them). 
S V C

(それをもらって) (本当に) 驚きました。

⑤ Also, Mom borrowed a video camera (from her friend).
S V O

また，ママが (友人から) ビデオカメラを借りました。

⑥ She took a video, so you will be able to see it all.
S① V① O① S② V② O②

ママが動画を撮ったので，おばあちゃんはそれを全部見られるでしょう。

⑦ She'll send it (to you) (soon).
S V O

ママが (すぐに) (おばあちゃんに) それを送ります。

⑧ I hope [you will enjoy it].
S V OS' V' O'

[それを楽しんでもらえる] といいなと思います。

注1　この文での to 不定詞は「V して」という意味で，直前の happy という気持ちになった理由を示すために使われています。

注2　文頭の It は仮主語で，後ろの that S V という節を指しています。that は接続詞で，that S V で「S が V すること」という意味の名詞のカタマリを作るために使われています。

注3　who は関係代名詞で，それに続く部分は直前の a friend of mine という名詞を修飾しています。

注4　この文での to 不定詞は「V して」という意味で，直前の surprised という気持ちになった理由を示すために使われています。

Unit 7

サイトトランスレーション

⇒別冊 p.12 ~ 13

1 Dear Grandma, /	おばあちゃんへ,
Thank you very much /	ありがとうございます
for the birthday money. //	誕生日祝いのお金を。
I was planning /	私は計画していました
to buy /	買おうと
a new soccer ball or a watch, /	新しいサッカーボールか腕時計を,
but I saw /	けれど目に入りました
a video game, /	テレビゲームが,
and I bought that. //	そしてそれを買いました。
It’s really fun, /	それは本当に楽しいです,
but Mom says /	でもママは言います
I can only play it /	私はそれで遊べるだけだ
for 30 minutes /	30 分間
every day. //	毎日。
I’m busy /	私は忙しいです
because I have to practice the clarinet /	クラリネットを練習しなくてはならないので
for our school concert. //	校内コンサートのために。
We practice /	私たちは練習します
for one hour /	1 時間
in the morning. //	朝。
Then after school /	それから放課後に

we have another practice /	私たちはさらに練習があります
for 90 minutes. //	90 分間。
Can you come /	おばあちゃんは来ることができますか
to the concert? //	コンサートに。
It will be on Saturday, October 2. //	それは 10 月 2 日，土曜日にあります。
It will start /	それは始まる予定です
at 2:00 p.m., /	午後 2 時に，
and it will be about two hours long. //	そして約 2 時間の長さの予定です。
Love, /	それでは，
Wendy //	ウェンディ
2 Dear Wendy, /	ウェンディへ，
I'm happy /	私はうれしいです
to hear /	聞いて
you're enjoying /	あなたが楽しんでいると
the video game. //	テレビゲームを。
It's great /	すばらしいことです
that you're practicing /	あなたが練習しているのは
the clarinet /	クラリネットを
so much. //	それほどたくさん。
I want to go /	私は行きたいです
to your concert, /	あなたのコンサートに，
but I will travel /	でも旅行するつもりです
to Weston /	ウェストンへ
that weekend. //	その週末には。

I'm going to visit /	私は訪問する予定です
a friend of mine /	友人を
who lives there. //	そこに住んでいる。
I already bought /	私はもう買いました
tickets, /	チケットを,
so I can't change /	だから変更することができません
my plans. //	計画を。
I know /	私は知っています
that you're a great clarinet player, /	あなたがクラリネットがとても上手なことは,
so I'm sure /	だからきっと…でしょう
the concert will be very good. //	コンサートは大変すてきなものになる。
Love, /	ではまた,
Grandma //	おばあちゃん
3 Dear Grandma, /	おばあちゃんへ,
I played /	私は演奏しました
in the concert /	コンサートで
today! //	今日！
I was nervous, /	私は緊張しました,
but everybody clapped /	でもみんな拍手してくれました
a lot /	たくさん
for our performance. //	私たちの演奏に。
Thank you /	ありがとう
for sending /	送ってくれて
the flowers. //	花を。

I was really surprised /	私は本当に驚きました
to get them. //	それをもらって。
Also, /	また,
Mom borrowed /	ママが借りました
a video camera /	ビデオカメラを
from her friend. //	ママの友達から。
She took a video, /	ママは動画を撮りました,
so you will be able to /	だからおばあちゃんはできます
see it all. //	それを全部見る。
She'll send it /	ママがそれを送ります
to you /	おばあちゃんに
soon. //	すぐに。
I hope /	私はいいなと思います
you will enjoy it. //	おばあちゃんがそれを楽しんでくれると。
Love, /	またね,
Wendy //	ウェンディ

問題英文と全訳

⇒別冊 p.12 ～ 13

From: Wendy Pierce
To: Barbara Pierce
Date: September 22
Subject: Thank you

Dear Grandma,
Thank you very much for the birthday money. I was planning to buy a new soccer ball or a watch, but I saw a video game, and I bought that. It's really fun, but Mom says I can only play it for 30 minutes every day. I'm busy because I have to practice the clarinet for our school concert. We practice for one hour in the morning. Then after school, we have another practice for 90 minutes. Can you come to the concert? It will be on Saturday, October 2. It will start at 2:00 p.m., and it will be about two hours long.
Love,
Wendy

送信者：ウェンディ・ピアス
受信者：バーバラ・ピアス
日付：9 月 22 日
件名：ありがとう

おばあちゃんへ
誕生日祝いのお金をありがとうございます。新しいサッカーボールか腕時計を買おうと計画していたけれど，テレビゲームが目に入り，それを買いました。それは本当に楽しいけれど，毎日 30 分しかしてはいけないとママは言います。私は校内コンサートのためにクラリネットを練習しなければならないので忙しいです。私たちは朝 1 時間練習します。それから放課後にもう 90 分間の練習があります。コンサートに来ることはできますか。10 月 2 日の土曜日にあります。午後 2 時に始まって，約 2 時間かかる予定です。
それでは，
ウェンディ

From: Barbara Pierce
To: Wendy Pierce
Date: September 25
Subject: Concert

Dear Wendy,

I'm happy to hear you're enjoying the video game. It's great that you're practicing the clarinet so much. I want to go to your concert, but I will travel to Weston that weekend. I'm going to visit a friend of mine who lives there. I already bought tickets, so I can't change my plans. I know that you're a great clarinet player, so I'm sure the concert will be very good.

Love,
Grandma

From: Wendy Pierce
To: Barbara Pierce
Date: October 2
Subject: All done!

Dear Grandma,

I played in the concert today! I was nervous, but everybody clapped a lot for our performance. Thank you for sending the flowers. I was really surprised to get them. Also, Mom borrowed a video camera from her friend. She took a video, so you will be able to see it all. She'll send it to you soon. I hope you will enjoy it.

Love,
Wendy

送信者：バーバラ・ピアス
受信者：ウェンディ・ピアス
日付：9月25日
件名：コンサート

ウェンディへ
あなたがテレビゲームを楽しんでいると聞いてうれしいです。クラリネットをそれほど練習しているのはすばらしいことです。あなたのコンサートに行きたいけれど，私はその週末にはウェストンへ旅行に行きます。そこに住んでいる友人を訪問する予定です。もう切符を買ったので，予定を変更できません。あなたのクラリネットがとても上手なことは知っているので，コンサートはきっと大変すてきなものになるでしょう。
ではまた，
おばあちゃん

送信者：ウェンディ・ピアス
受信者：バーバラ・ピアス
日付：10月2日
件名：すべて終えました！

おばあちゃんへ
今日コンサートで演奏しました！　緊張したけれど，みんな私たちの演奏にたくさん拍手してくれました。花を送ってくれてありがとう。それをもらって本当に驚きました。また，ママが友人からビデオカメラを借りました。ママが動画を撮ったので，おばあちゃんはそれを全部見られるでしょう。ママがすぐにそれを送ります。楽しんでもらえるといいなと思います。
またね，
ウェンディ

⇒別冊 p.14 ~ 15

解答と解説

解答

(1) ③　(2) ④　(3) ①

解説

(1) テレサの最初のメール（1つめのメール）の第1文後半のI am working on an article about you and your clothesと第3文後半のI would really like to ask you some questions about your workから考えて，**3**が正解。

設問・選択肢の和訳

(1) テレサはラルーさんに…について尋（たず）ねたいと思っている

× 1　ファッション雑誌を始めること。
× 2　彼女の衣料品店で働くこと。
○ 3　ファッション・デザイナーという彼女の仕事。
× 4　デザイン賞を誰が受賞するか。

(2) ソフィーのメール（2つめのメール）の第3・4文のI will have a fashion show on May 27. Two days after the fashion show, I am going on a trip to Paris.から考えて，**4**が正解。

設問・選択肢の和訳

(2) 5月29日に，ソフィー・ラルーは何をするか。

× 1　ファッション雑誌の記事を書く。
× 2　ファッションショーを開く。
× 3　打ち合わせに行く。
○ 4　パリへ旅行する。

(3) テレサの2回めのメール（3つめのメール）の最後の2文のThe next issue of the school newspaper will be published on Wednesday next week. I'll send you a copy then!から考えて，**1**が正解。

設問・選択肢の和訳

(3) テレサは来週何をするか。

○ 1　自分の記事を1部ソフィー・ラルーに送る。
× 2　再びソフィー・ラルーに電話する。
× 3　ソフィー・ラルーに自分の絵をあげる。
× 4　ソフィー・ラルーに関する記事を書き終える。

語句

DOWN LOAD

〈1つめのメール〉

- □ request　（名）願い，頼み
- □ article　（名）記事
- □ clothes　（名）衣服
- □ magazine　（名）雑誌
- □ award　（名）賞
- □ would like to *do*　～したい
- □ yours truly　敬具

〈2つめのメール〉

- □ right now　ちょうど今
- □ go on a trip to ～　～へ旅行する
- □ sincerely　（副）敬具

〈3つめのメール〉

- □ drawing　（名）（線で描いた）絵
- □ next to ～　～の隣に
- □ copy　（名）（印刷物などの）1部

構造確認 ※誤読した部分の確認に使用してください。

⇒別冊 p.14 ~ 15

1つめのメール テレサ・ピアソンからソフィー・ラルーへ／件名：お願い

① I am a writer 〈for the Pennington High School newspaper〉, and I am working (on an article 〈about you and your clothes〉).

私は〈ペニントン高校新聞の〉ライターで，(〈あなたとあなたの服に関する〉記事に) 取り組んでいます。

② I read (in a magazine) [that you won the Young Fashion Designer of the Year award (this year)], and I thought [your clothes were beautiful].

[あなたが (今年) ヤング・ファッション・デザイナー年間最優秀賞を獲得されたこと] を (雑誌で) 読み，私は [あなたの服は美しい] と思いました。

③ I know [that you are very busy], but I would (really) like to ask you some questions 〈about your work〉.

私は [あなたが非常に忙しいということ] は知っていますが，あなたに (ぜひ)〈あなたのお仕事に関しての〉いくつかの質問をしたいです。

④ I would like to talk (to you) (for about 10 minutes) (on the phone).

(電話で) (あなたと) (約 10 分間) お話ししたいです。

2つめのメール ソフィー・ラルーからテレサ・ピアソンへ／件名：あなたのご依頼

① Thank you (for your e-mail).

(メールをいただき) ありがとうございます。

② I was happy (to hear [that you read (about me) (in the magazine)]).

([あなたが (私のことを) (雑誌で) 読んだ] と聞いて) 私はうれしく思いました。

③ I'm very busy (right now) (because I will have a fashion show (on May 27)).

((5月27日に) ファッションショーがあるため) 私は (ちょうど今) とても忙しいです。

④ (Two days after the fashion show), I am going (on a trip to Paris). 

(ファッションショーの2日後に), (パリへ旅行) します。

⑤ I am free (only on May 28).

私は (5月28日だけ) 空いています。

⑥ I will have meetings (in the morning), but you could call me (in the afternoon).

(午前中は) 打ち合わせがありますが, (午後は) 私に電話してもかまいません。

⑦ My phone number is 555-2985.

私の電話番号は555-2985です。

3つめのメール テレサ・ピアソンからソフィー・ラルーへ／件名：ありがとうございます

① Thank you so much (for [talking to me yesterday])!

([昨日私と話していただいたこと] に) 大変感謝します (ありがとうございます) !

② And thank you (also) (for the drawings 〈you gave me〉). 

そして (〈私にくださった〉絵に) (も) 感謝します。

③ We're going to put them (in the newspaper) (next to the article).

それらは (新聞の) (記事の隣に) 入れる予定です。

④ I think [the article is going to be (really) interesting].
S V O S' V' C'

[その記事は (本当に) おもしろくなる] と思います。

⑤ I will finish [writing it] (this weekend).
S V O

(今週末に) [それを書き] 終えるでしょう。

⑥ The next issue 〈of the school newspaper〉 will be published (on Wednesday next week).
S V

次号〈の学校新聞〉は (来週水曜日に) 発行されます。

⑦ I'll send you a copy (then)!
S V O O

(そのとき) 1 部をあなたにお送りします！

注1 前置詞＋名詞 は，直前の名詞を修飾する働きをすることもできます。この文では，about から clothes までの部分が直前の an article を修飾する働きをしています。

注2 would like to V は「V したいです」という意味で，want to V よりもていねいな表現です。会話やメールでよく使われます。

注3 この文のように，確定している予定を表す場合には，現在進行形や現在形が使われることがあります。

注4 you gave me の部分が直前の the drawings という名詞を修飾しています。drawings の直後に，関係代名詞の that もしくは which が省略されていると考えるとよいでしょう。

Unit 8

サイトトランスレーション

⇒別冊 p.14 ~ 15

1 Dear Ms. LaRue, /	拝啓（はいけい） ラルー様,
I am a writer /	私はライターです
for the Pennington High School newspaper, /	ペニントン高校新聞の,
and I am working on /	私は取り組んでいます
an article /	記事に
about you and your clothes. //	あなたとあなたの服に関する。
I read /	私は読みました
in a magazine /	雑誌で
that you won /	あなたが獲得されたことを
the Young Fashion Designer of the Year award /	ヤング・ファッション・デザイナー年間最優秀賞を
this year, /	今年の,
and I thought /	そして私は思いました
your clothes were beautiful. //	あなたの服は美しいと。
I know /	私は承知しています
that you are very busy, /	あなたが非常にお忙しいことを,
but I would really like to ask you /	けれどぜひ尋ねたいと思っています
some questions /	いくつかの質問を
about your work. //	あなたのお仕事に関しての。
I would like to talk to you /	私はあなたとお話しさせていただければと思います
for about 10 minutes /	約 10 分間
on the phone. //	電話で。
Yours Truly, /	敬具,

Teresa Pearson //	テレサ・ピアソン
2 Dear Teresa, /	拝啓 テレサ様,
Thank you /	ありがとうございます
for your e-mail. //	メールをいただいて。
I was happy to hear /	私は聞いてうれしく思いました
that you read /	あなたが読んだと
about me /	私のことを
in the magazine. //	雑誌で。
I'm very busy /	私はとても忙しいです
right now /	ちょうど今
because I will have a fashion show /	ファッションショーがあるため
on May 27. //	5月27日に。
Two days after the fashion show, /	ファッションショーの2日後に,
I am going on a trip /	私は旅行する予定です
to Paris. //	パリへ。
I am free /	私は空いています
only on May 28. //	5月28日だけ。
I will have meetings /	私は打ち合わせがあります
in the morning, /	午前中は,
but you could call me /	でも電話をしていただいてもかまいません
in the afternoon. //	午後は。
My phone number is /	私の電話番号は…です
555-2985. //	555-2985。
Sincerely, /	敬具,
Sophie LaRue //	ソフィー・ラルー

3 Dear Ms. LaRue, /	拝啓 ラルー様,
Thank you so much /	大変ありがとうございます
for talking to me /	私と話していただいて
yesterday! //	昨日は！
And thank you also /	そしてまた感謝します
for the drawings /	絵に
you gave me. //	あなたが私にくださった。
We're going to put them /	それらを入れる予定です
in the newspaper /	新聞の中の
next to the article. //	その記事の隣に。
I think /	私は思います
the article is going to be /	記事はなるでしょう
really interesting. //	本当におもしろく。
I will finish writing it /	私はそれを書き終えるでしょう
this weekend. //	今週末に。
The next issue of the school newspaper /	次号の学校新聞は
will be published /	発行されます
on Wednesday /	水曜日に
next week. //	来週の。
I'll send /	私は送るでしょう
you /	あなたに
a copy /	1部
then! //	そのとき！
Yours Truly, /	敬具,
Teresa Pearson //	テレサ・ピアソン

問題英文と全訳

⇒別冊 p.14 ～ 15

From: Teresa Pearson
To: Sophie LaRue
Date: May 9
Subject: Request

Dear Ms. LaRue,
I am a writer for the Pennington High School newspaper, and I am working on an article about you and your clothes. I read in a magazine that you won the Young Fashion Designer of the Year award this year, and I thought your clothes were beautiful. I know that you are very busy, but I would really like to ask you some questions about your work. I would like to talk to you for about 10 minutes on the phone.
Yours Truly,
Teresa Pearson

送信者：テレサ・ピアソン
受信者：ソフィー・ラルー
日付：5月9日
件名：お願い

拝啓 ラルー様
私はペニントン高校新聞のライターで，あなたとあなたの服に関する記事に取り組んでいます。あなたが今年のヤング・ファッション・デザイナー年間最優秀賞を獲得されたことを雑誌で読み，私はあなたの服を美しいと思いました。非常にお忙しいことは承知していますが，あなたのお仕事に関してぜひいくつか質問させていただきたいと思っています。電話で約10分間，あなたとお話をさせていただければと思います。
敬具
テレサ・ピアソン

From: Sophie LaRue
To: Teresa Pearson
Date: May 10
Subject: Your request

Dear Teresa,
Thank you for your e-mail. I was happy to hear that you read about me in the magazine. I'm very busy right now because I will have a fashion show on May 27. Two days after the fashion show, I am going on a trip to Paris. I am free only on May 28. I will have meetings in the morning, but you could call me in the afternoon. My phone number is 555-2985.
Sincerely,
Sophie LaRue

From: Teresa Pearson
To: Sophie LaRue
Date: May 29
Subject: Thank you

Dear Ms. LaRue,
Thank you so much for talking to me yesterday! And thank you also for the drawings you gave me. We're going to put them in the newspaper next to the article. I think the article is going to be really interesting. I will finish writing it this weekend. The next issue of the school newspaper will be published on Wednesday next week. I'll send you a copy then!
Yours Truly,
Teresa Pearson

送信者：ソフィー・ラルー
受信者：テレサ・ピアソン
日付：5月10日
件名：あなたのご依頼

拝啓 テレサ様
メールをいただき，ありがとうございます。私のことを雑誌で読んだと聞いてうれしく思いました。5月27日にファッションショーがあるため，私はちょうど今とても忙しいです。ファッションショーの2日後に，パリへ旅行します。5月28日だけ空いています。午前中は打ち合わせがありますが，午後なら電話をしていただいてもかまいません。私の電話番号は555-2985です。
敬具
ソフィー・ラルー

送信者：テレサ・ピアソン
受信者：ソフィー・ラルー
日付：5月29日
件名：ありがとうございます

拝啓 ラルー様
昨日は私と話していただき，大変ありがとうございます！　また，くださった絵にも感謝します。それらは新聞記事の隣に入れる予定です。記事は本当におもしろくなると思います。それは今週末には書き終わります。次号の学校新聞は来週水曜日に発行されます。そのとき1部をあなたにお送りします！
敬具
テレサ・ピアソン

⇒別冊 p.16 ~ 17

解答と解説

解答

(1) ③　(2) ①　(3) ④

解説

(1) ローラからの最初のメール（1つめのメール）の第5文に Green Mountain is a great resort, but it's a long way from my house. とあるので，**3** が正解。

設問・選択肢の和訳

(1) ローラは，グリーン山スキー場は…と言う
×1 2月は無料でスキーができる。
×2 彼女の大好きなスキー場だ。
○3 彼女の家から遠い。
×4 午前8時に営業を開始する。

(2) マーラからのメール（2つめのメール）の第2文に I can go on February 14, but I have to visit my grandma's house on the other day. とある。下線部の「(14日ではなく) もう一方の日」とは，ローラからの最初のメールの第4文の We can go on February 7 or 14. から考えて，2月7日である。したがって，**1** が正解。

設問・選択肢の和訳

(2) マーラは2月7日スキーに行くことができない，なぜなら…
○1 彼女は祖母に会わなければならない。
×2 彼女は買い物に行かなければならない。
×3 彼女の兄がスキー板を必要としている。
×4 スキー場が閉まっている。

(3) ローラからの2回めのメール（3つめのメール）の最後の文に Could you bring it again this time? とあり，it とは前の文中の a nice camera のことだから，**4** が正解。

設問・選択肢の和訳

(3) ローラはマーラに…を持ってくるよう頼んでいる
×1 暖かいセーター。
×2 お金。
×3 食べ物。
○4 カメラ。

語句

DOWN LOAD

〈1 つめのメール〉

☐ ski resort スキー場

☐ Would you like to *do*? ～しませんか

☐ resort （名）行楽地

☐ a long way from ～ ～から遠い

☐ around （前）～ごろ

☐ all day 一日中

〈2 つめのメール〉

☐ while （接）～する間

☐ come shopping 買い物に来る

〈3 つめのメール〉

☐ mall （名）（ショッピング）モール

☐ sweater （名）セーター

☐ pay for ～ ～の代金を払う

☐ lift （名）（スキー場の）リフト

Column ほどほどに文法を学ぼう！

英語の長文が読めるようになるためには，日本語の解説を読むことも大切かもしれませんが，やはり英語をたくさん読むことが大切です。本書にも，わからないところを確認するために「構造確認」というページが設けてありますが，そこで示しているように隅（すみ）から隅まで英文が分解できなければならないというわけではありません。あくまでも，わからないところの確認用に使ってください。文法をしっかり学んでから，長文を読むというよりは，長文を読むことを楽しみながら，同時に文法の力もつけていきましょう。

4 技能試験には，あまり文法問題は出題されませんが，文法の力は大切です。動詞をどのように使うのか，また，関係代名詞や準動詞などはどのような働きをするのかといった知識は，4 技能を習得していくために避けては通れません。しかし，分厚い文法の本を隅から隅まで読んだり，文法の問題をたくさん解いたりするような勉強よりも，実際に使う大切なルールにしぼり込んで，例文を音読し，暗唱しながら学ぶことが，これからは大切です。

単語を覚えるときにも，やはり例文を音読しながら覚えることが大切です。単語集を勉強するときにも，リストで単語だけを覚えるよりも，例文を読むことを重視して文中での使い方を勉強してください。本書にも，すべての英文に，単語集としても使える単語リストがついています。これらのリストも，いきなりリストを暗記するというよりは，長文の中で覚えたものを確認してチェックする形で学習を進めましょう。

構造確認 ※誤読した部分の確認に使用してください。

⇒別冊 p.16 ~ 17

1つめのメール ローラ・ヒギンズからマーラ・ブラントフォードへ／件名：グリーン山スキー場

① How are you?
C V S

お元気ですか。

② My parents and I are going (to Green Mountain Ski Resort) (next month).
S V

両親と私は (来月) (グリーン山スキー場に) 行く予定です。

③ (If you're free), would you like to come (with us)?
S' V' C' V S

(もし暇なら), (私たちと一緒に) 来ませんか。

④ We can go (on February 7 or 14).
S V

私たちは (2月7日か14日に) 行けます。

⑤ Green Mountain is a great resort, but it's a long way (from my house).
S① V① C① S② V② C②

グリーン山はすばらしい行楽地ですが, (私の家から) 遠いところにあります。

⑥ We're going to leave (at around 5:00 a.m.) and drive (until 8:00 a.m.)
S V① V②

私たちは (午前5時ごろ) 出発して (午前8時まで) 車で行くつもりです。

⑦ We'll ski (all day from 9:00 a.m.) and (then) leave the resort (at around 5:00 p.m.)
S V① V② O②

(午前9時から一日中) スキーをして (それから) (午後5時ごろ) スキー場を出発するつもりです。

⑧ We'll get (home) (at around 10:00 p.m.)
S V

(午後10時ごろに) (家に) 着くでしょう。

⑨ Please tell me [if you can come]. 
V O O S' V'

[あなたが来られるかどうか] 私に教えてください。

2つめのメール マーラ・ブラントフォードからローラ・ヒギンズへ／件名：行けます！

① Thanks (for [asking me]).

([私に聞いて] くれて) ありがとう。

② I can go (on February 14), but I have to visit my grandma's house (on the other day).
S① V① S② V② O②

(2月14日には) 行けますが，(もう一方の日には) 祖母の家を訪問しなければなりません。

③ I don't have any skis, but my older brother said [I could use his]. 
S① V① O① S② V② O② S' V' O'

私はスキー板を一つも持っていませんが，兄が [彼のものを使ってもいい] と言ってくれました。

④ I (also) want to buy a new ski jacket.
S V O

私は新しいスキージャケット (も) 買いたいです。

⑤ I want to look good (while I'm skiing)! 
S V C S' V'

(スキーをしている間) すてきに見えたいです！

⑥ Do you want to come shopping (with me) (this weekend)?
V S

(今週末に) (私と一緒に) 買い物にしに来ませんか。

3つめのメール ローラ・ヒギンズからマーラ・ブラントフォードへ／件名：買い物

① I'm glad you can come (with us)!
S V C S' V'

あなたが（私たちと一緒に）来られてうれしいです！

② And yes, I want to go (to the mall) (with you).
S V

それから了解(りょうかい)です，私は（あなたと一緒に）（モールへ）行きたいです。

③ I got $60 (for my birthday), so I want to buy a warm sweater.
S① V① O① S② V② O②

（誕生日に）60ドルもらったので，私は暖かいセーターを買いたいです。

④ Mom says [she can pay (for your lift ticket and food 〈at the ski resort〉)].
S V O S' V'

母が［（〈スキー場での〉あなたのリフト券と食事の）支払いをしてくれる］と言っています。

⑤ (Last time), you had a nice camera, and you took photos (with it).
S① V① O① S② V② O②

（前回），あなたはよいカメラを持っていて，（それで）写真を撮っていました。

⑥ Could you bring it (again) (this time)?
V S O

（今回）（また）それを持って来てくれませんか。

注1 この文での if は「もしも…ならば」という意味で使われています。⑨の文の if と比較してみましょう。

注2 この文での if は「もしも…ならば」という意味ではありません。if S V という形で名詞の働きをし，「S が V するかどうか」という意味を表しています。

注3 主文の動詞の said が過去形であるのに合わせて，それに続く節でも can の過去形の could が使われています。このように，動詞の時制はふつう一致させます。

注4 while は接続詞です。while S V で「S が V する間」「S が V しながら」という意味になります。

注5 Could you V? は「V してもらえませんか」という意味で，ていねいにお願い事をする場合によく使う表現です。

Unit 9

サイトトランスレーション

⇒別冊 p.16 ~ 17

1 Hi Marla, /	こんにちは，マーラ，
How are you? //	お元気ですか。
My parents and I are going /	両親と私は行きます
to Green Mountain Ski Resort /	グリーン山スキー場に
next month. //	来月。
If you're free, /	もしあなたが暇なら，
would you like to come /	来ませんか
with us? //	私たちと一緒に。
We can go /	私たちは行けます
on February 7 or 14. //	2月7日か14日に。
Green Mountain is a great resort, /	グリーン山はすばらしい行楽地です，
but it's a long way /	しかし遠いところにあります
from my house. //	私の家からは。
We're going to leave /	私たちは出発するつもりです
at around 5:00 a.m. /	午前5時ごろ
and drive /	そして車で行きます
until 8:00 a.m. //	午前8時まで。
We'll ski /	私たちはスキーをします
all day /	一日中
from 9:00 a.m. /	午前9時から
and then leave /	それから出発します

the resort /	スキー場を
at around 5:00 p.m. //	午後５時ごろ。
We'll get home /	私たちは家に着くでしょう
at around 10:00 p.m. //	午後 10 時ごろ。
Please tell me /	私に教えてください
if you can come. //	あなたが来られるかどうか。
Your friend, /	よろしく，
Laura //	ローラ
2 Hi Laura, /	こんにちは，ローラ，
Thanks /	ありがとう
for asking me. //	私に聞いてくれて。
I can go /	私は行けます
on February 14, /	２月 14 日に，
but I have to visit /	でも訪問しなければなりません
my grandma's house /	祖母の家を
on the other day. //	もう一方の日は。
I don't have /	私は持っていません
any skis, /	スキー板を一つも，
but my older brother said /	でも兄が言いました
I could use /	使ってもいいと
his. //	彼のものを。
I also want to buy /	私はまた買いたいです
a new ski jacket. //	新しいスキージャケットを。
I want to look good /	私はすてきに見えたいです

while I'm skiing! //	スキーをしている間！
Do you want to come shopping /	買い物にしに行きませんか
with me /	私と一緒に
this weekend? //	今週末に。
Your friend, /	よろしく，
Marla //	マーラ
3 Hi Marla, /	こんにちは，マーラ，
I'm glad /	うれしいです
you can come /	あなたが来られて
with us! //	私たちと一緒に！
And yes, /	それから了解です，
I want to go /	私は行きたいです
to the mall /	モールへ
with you. //	あなたと一緒に。
I got $60 /	私は 60 ドルもらいました
for my birthday, /	誕生日に，
so I want to buy /	だから買いたいです
a warm sweater. //	暖かいセーターを。
Mom says /	母が言っています
she can pay /	払ってくれると
for your lift ticket and food /	あなたのリフト券と食事代を
at the ski resort. //	スキー場での。
Last time, /	前回，
you had a nice camera, /	あなたはよいカメラを持っていました，

and you took photos with it. //	そしてそれで写真を撮っていました。
Could you bring it /	それを持って来てくれませんか
again this time? //	今回もまた。
Your friend, /	よろしく,
Laura //	ローラ

問題英文と全訳

⇒別冊 p.16 ~ 17

From: Laura Higgins
To: Marla Brantford
Date: January 14
Subject: Green Mountain Ski Resort

Hi Marla,
How are you? My parents and I are going to Green Mountain Ski Resort next month. If you're free, would you like to come with us? We can go on February 7 or 14. Green Mountain is a great resort, but it's a long way from my house. We're going to leave at around 5:00 a.m. and drive until 8:00 a.m. We'll ski all day from 9:00 a.m. and then leave the resort at around 5:00 p.m. We'll get home at around 10:00 p.m. Please tell me if you can come.
Your friend,
Laura

送信者：ローラ・ヒギンズ
受信者：マーラ・ブラントフォード
日付：1月14日
件名：グリーン山スキー場

こんにちは，マーラ
お元気ですか。来月，両親と私でグリーン山スキー場に行きます。もし暇なら私たちと一緒に来ませんか。2月7日か14日に行けます。グリーン山はすばらしい行楽地ですが，私の家からは遠いところにあります。私たちは午前5時ごろ出発して，午前8時まで車で行きます。午前9時から一日中スキーをして，それから午後5時ごろスキー場を出発します。午後10時ごろに家に着くでしょう。来られるかどうか私に教えてください。
よろしく，
ローラ

From: Marla Brantford
To: Laura Higgins
Date: January 15
Subject: I can go!

Hi Laura,
Thanks for asking me. I can go on February 14, but I have to visit my grandma's house on the other day. I don't have any skis, but my older brother said I could use his. I also want to buy a new ski jacket. I want to look good while I'm skiing! Do you want to come shopping with me this weekend?
Your friend,
Marla

From: Laura Higgins
To: Marla Brantford
Date: January 15
Subject: Shopping

Hi Marla,
I'm glad you can come with us! And yes, I want to go to the mall with you. I got $60 for my birthday, so I want to buy a warm sweater. Mom says she can pay for your lift ticket and food at the ski resort. Last time, you had a nice camera, and you took photos with it. Could you bring it again this time?
Your friend,
Laura

送信者：マーラ・ブラントフォード
受信者：ローラ・ヒギンズ
日付：1 月 15 日
件名：行けます！

こんにちは，ローラ
私に聞いてくれてありがとう。2 月 14 日は行けますが，もう一方の日は祖母の家を訪問しなければなりません。スキー板を一つも持っていませんが，兄が自分のを使ってもいいと言ってくれました。新しいスキージャケットも買いたいです。スキーをしている間，すてきに見えたいです！　今週末に一緒に買い物にしに来ませんか。
よろしく，
マーラ

送信者：ローラ・ヒギンズ
受信者：マーラ・ブラントフォード
日付：1 月 15 日
件名：買い物

こんにちは，マーラ
あなたが一緒に来られてうれしいです！　それから了解です，一緒にモールへ行きたいです。誕生日に 60 ドルもらったので，私は暖かいセーターを買いたいです。母がスキー場でのあなたのリフト券と食事代を払ってくれると言っています。前回あなたはよいカメラを持っていて，それで写真を撮っていました。今回もまた，それを持って来てくれませんか。
よろしく，
ローラ

⇒別冊 p.18 ~ 19

解答と解説

解答

(1) ④　(2) ①　(3) ①

解説

(1) メラニーの最初のメール(1つめのメール)の第4文の後半に I moved to Springfield at the beginning of last month とあるので,**4**が正解。

設問・選択肢の和訳

(1) メラニーはいつスプリングフィールドに来たか。

×1 昨日。　×2 5年前。　×3 この前の日曜日。　○4 1か月前。

(2) メラニーの最初のメール(1つめのメール)の最後の文に I'd like to join you. とあるので,**1**が正解。

設問・選択肢の和訳

(2) メラニーは何をしたいか。

○1 ダンのバンドに加わる。　×2 ダンのコンサートのチケットを手に入れる。
×3 自分のギターをダンに売る。　×4 ダンの楽器店で働く。

(3) メラニーの2回めのメール(3つめのメール)の第2文の I'd like to come on Wednesday とダンのメール(2つめのメール)の第6・7文の We have practices on Tuesday, Wednesday, and Friday from 7:00 p.m. to 9:00 p.m. We practice at the Springfield Community Center, in Room 208. から考えて,**1**が正解。

設問・選択肢の和訳

(3) 今度の水曜日にメラニーは何をするか。

○1 スプリングフィールド公民館に行く。　×2 新しい歌を書く。
×3 自分のコンサートのために練習する。　×4 ダンのホームページ用に新しいデザインを作る。

語句

DOWN LOAD

〈1つめのメール〉

- □ poster　(名) ポスター,貼(は)り紙
- □ during　(前) ～の間
- □ move　(動) 引っ越す
- □ at the beginning of ～　～の初めに
- □ usually　(副) いつも,ふだん
- □ rock and pop music　ロックとポップス
- □ I'd like to *do*　～したい

〈2つめのメール〉

- □ invite　(動) ～を誘う
- □ would like O to *do*　Oに～してもらいたい
- □ practice　(名) 練習　(動) ～を練習する
- □ website　(名) ホームページ

〈3つめのメール〉

- □ A called B　Bと呼ばれるA,BというA
- □ myself　(代) 自分自身で

構造確認 ※誤読した部分の確認に使用してください。

⇒別冊 p.18 ～ 19

1つめのメール メラニー・ジョーンズからダン・キャンベルへ／件名：あなたのポスター

① I saw your poster (at Super Sounds Music Store) (last Sunday).
S V O

(この前の日曜日に) (スーパー・サウンド楽器店で) あなたのポスターを見ました。

② It says [that your band needs a new guitar player].
S V O S' V' O'

それには [あなたのバンドが新しいギター奏者を求めている] と書いてありますね。

③ I started [playing the guitar] (five years ago).
S V O

私は (5年前) [ギターを弾き] 始めました。

④ I was (in a band) (during high school), but I moved (to Springfield) (at the beginning 〈of last month〉).
S① V① S② V②

(高校の間) (バンドに入って) いましたが，(〈先月の〉初めに) (スプリングフィールドに) 引っ越しました。

⑤ Now I'm a college student, and I want to find a new band and play (with new members).
S① V① C① S② V② O② V③

今私は大学生で，新しいバンドを見つけて，(新しいメンバーと) 演奏したいと思っています。

⑥ I (usually) play rock and pop music.
S V O

私は (いつも) ロックとポップスを演奏します。

⑦ I'd like to join you.
S V O

あなたたちのバンドに入りたいと思っています。

2つめのメール ダン・キャンベルからメラニー・ジョーンズへ／件名：こんにちは

① Thanks (for your e-mail).

(メールを) ありがとうございます。

② All the members 〈of our band〉 go (to Springfield University).

〈僕たちのバンドの〉メンバー全員が (スプリングフィールド大学に) 通っています。

③ Is that the university 〈you go to〉?

それは〈あなたが通っている〉大学ですか。

④ I got e-mails (from three people 〈who want to be (in our band)〉), so we're inviting everyone and will listen to you all play (for us) (this week).

(〈(うちのバンドに) 入りたいという〉3人から) メールをもらったので，みんなを誘って，(今週) あなたたち全員が (僕たちに) 演奏するのを聞くつもりです。

⑤ We would like you to come (to play for us).

僕たちはあなたに (僕たちのために演奏をしに) 来てほしいです。

⑥ We have practices (on Tuesday, Wednesday, and Friday from 7:00 p.m. to 9:00 p.m.)

僕たちは (火，水，金曜日の午後7時から午後9時まで) 練習があります。

⑦ We practice (at the Springfield Community Center), (in Room 208).

僕たちは (スプリングフィールド公民館の)，(208号室で) 練習しています。

⑧ Which is the best day 〈for you〉?
V S

〈あなたにとって〉最もよい日はいつですか。

⑨ (After all three people have played (for us)), we'll invite one person.
S' V' S V O

(3人全員が (僕たちのために) 演奏した後で), 僕たちは1人を誘うつもりです。

⑩ You can listen to our music (on our website).
S V

(ホームページで) 僕たちの音楽を聞くことができます。

⑪ The address is www.springfieldfive.com.
S V C

アドレスは www.springfieldfive.com です。

3つめのメール メラニー・ジョーンズからダン・キャンベルへ／件名：すばらしい音楽

① I think [your music is great].
S V O S' V' C'

[あなたたちの音楽はすばらしい] と思います。

② I'd like to come (on Wednesday).
S V

(水曜日に) そちらへ行きたいです。

③ I've been practicing a song 〈called "Maybe Tomorrow"〉. 注3
S V O

私は〈『メイビー・トゥモロー』という〉歌を練習しています。

④ It's a song 〈that I wrote myself〉.
S V C S' V'

それは〈私が自分で書いた〉歌です。

⑤ I hope [you like it].
S V O S' V' O'

[あなたがそれを気に入ってくれたら] いいなと思います。

⑥ I'm excited (to meet you and the other members 〈of your band〉).
S V C

(あなたと〈あなたのバンドの〉他のメンバーの皆さんとお会いできることに) わくわくしています。

注1　ポスターなどに「書いてある」という意味を表現する場合には，say という動詞が使われます。この文では，that 以下の内容がポスターに書いてあったことを意味しています。(that) S V で「S が V すること」という意味の名詞の働きをするカタマリを作ることができます。

注2　would like 人 to V は「人に V してほしい」という意味の表現です。want 人 to V も同じような意味ですが，would like を使った方がていねいな言い方になります。

注3　A called B は「B と呼ばれる A」という意味です。called は過去分詞で，「〜される」「〜された」という意味で直前の名詞を修飾することができます。

Unit 10

サイトトランスレーション

⇒別冊 p.18 ~ 19

1 Dear Dan, /	ダンさんへ,
I saw /	私は見ました
your poster /	あなたのポスターを
at Super Sounds Music Store /	スーパー・サウンド楽器店で
last Sunday. //	この前の日曜日に。
It says /	それには書いてあります
that your band needs /	あなたのバンドが求めていると
a new guitar player. //	新しいギター奏者を。
I started playing the guitar /	私はギターを弾き始めました
five years ago. //	5年前。
I was in a band /	私はバンドに入っていました
during high school, /	高校の間,
but I moved /	けれど引っ越しました
to Springfield /	スプリングフィールドに
at the beginning of last month. //	先月の初めに。
Now /	今
I'm a college student, /	私は大学生です,
and I want to find /	そして見つけたいと思っています
a new band /	新しいバンドを
and play with new members. //	そして新しいメンバーと一緒に演奏する。
I usually play /	私はいつも演奏します

rock and pop music. //	ロックとポップスを。
I'd like to join /	私は加わりたいと思っています
you. //	あなたたち（のバンド）に。
Melanie //	メラニー
2 Dear Melanie, /	メラニーさんへ，
Thanks /	ありがとうございます
for your e-mail. //	メールを。
All the members /	メンバーは全員
of our band /	僕たちのバンドの
go to Springfield University. //	スプリングフィールド大学に通っています。
Is that the university /	それは大学ですか
you go to? //	あなたが通っている。
I got /	僕はもらいました
e-mails /	メールを
from three people /	3人から
who want to be in our band, /	僕たちのバンドに入りたいという，
so we're inviting /	なので僕たちは誘っています
everyone /	みんなを
and will listen to you all /	そしてあなたたち全員が～するのを聞くつもりです
play for us /	僕たちのために演奏する
this week. //	今週。
We would like you to come /	僕たちはあなたに来てほしいと思います
to play for us. //	僕たちのために演奏をしに。
We have practices /	僕たちは練習があります

on Tuesday, Wednesday, and Friday /	火，水，金曜日の
from 7:00 p.m. to 9:00 p.m. //	午後７時から午後９時まで。
We practice /	僕たちは練習しています
at the Springfield Community Center, /	スプリングフィールド公民館の,
in Room 208. //	208 号室で。
Which is /	どれですか
the best day /	最も都合のいい日は
for you? //	あなたにとって。
After /	後で
all three people have played /	３人全員が演奏した
for us, /	僕たちのために,
we'll invite /	僕たちは誘います
one person. //	１人を。
You can listen to /	あなたは聴くことができます
our music /	僕たちの音楽を
on our website. //	ホームページで。
The address is /	アドレスは…です
www.springfieldfive.com. //	www.springfieldfive.com.
Dan //	ダン
3 Dear Dan, /	ダンさんへ,
I think /	私は思います
your music is great. //	あなたたちの音楽はすばらしいと。
I'd like to come /	私は行きたいです
on Wednesday. //	水曜日に。

I've been practicing /	私は練習しています
a song /	歌を
called "Maybe Tomorrow." //	『メイビー・トゥモロー』という。
It's a song /	それは歌です
that I wrote myself. //	私が自分で書いた。
I hope /	私はいいなと思います
you like it. //	それを気に入っていただけると。
I'm excited /	私はわくわくしています
to meet /	お会いできることに
you and the other members /	あなたと他のメンバーの皆さんと
of your band. //	あなたのバンドの。
Melanie //	メラニー

問題英文と全訳

⇒別冊 p.18 ~ 19

From: Melanie Jones
To: Dan Campbell
Date: October 1
Subject: Your poster

Dear Dan,
I saw your poster at Super Sounds Music Store last Sunday. It says that your band needs a new guitar player. I started playing the guitar five years ago. I was in a band during high school, but I moved to Springfield at the beginning of last month. Now I'm a college student, and I want to find a new band and play with new members. I usually play rock and pop music. I'd like to join you.
Melanie

送信者：メラニー・ジョーンズ
受信者：ダン・キャンベル
日付：10月1日
件名：あなたのポスター

ダンさんへ
この前の日曜日に，スーパー・サウンド楽器店であなたのポスターを見ました。それには，あなたのバンドが新しいギター奏者を求めていると書いてありますね。私は5年前ギターを弾き始めました。高校の間バンドに入っていましたが，先月の初めにスプリングフィールドに引っ越しました。今私は大学生で，新しいバンドを見つけて，新しいメンバーと一緒に演奏したいと思っています。ふだんロックとポップスを演奏しています。あなたたちのバンドに入りたいと思っています。
メラニー

From: Dan Campbell
To: Melanie Jones
Date: October 1
Subject: Hello

Dear Melanie,
Thanks for your e-mail. All the members of our band go to Springfield University. Is that the university you go to? I got e-mails from three people who want to be in our band, so we're inviting everyone and will listen to you all play for us this week. We would like you to come to play for us. We have practices on Tuesday, Wednesday, and Friday from 7:00 p.m. to 9:00 p.m. We practice at the Springfield Community Center, in Room 208. Which is the best day for you? After all three people have played for us, we'll invite one person. You can listen to our music on our website. The address is www.springfieldfive.com.
Dan

From: Melanie Jones
To: Dan Campbell
Date: October 1
Subject: Great music

Dear Dan,
I think your music is great. I'd like to come on Wednesday. I've been practicing a song called "Maybe Tomorrow." It's a song that I wrote myself. I hope you like it. I'm excited to meet you and the other members of your band.
Melanie

送信者：ダン・キャンベル
受信者：メラニー・ジョーンズ
日付：10 月 1 日
件名：こんにちは

メラニーさんへ
メールをありがとうございます。僕たちのバンドのメンバーは全員スプリングフィールド大学に通っています。そこはあなたが通っている大学ですか。僕たちのバンドに入りたいという 3 人からメールをもらったので，みんなを誘って，今週あなたたち全員に僕たちに演奏を聞かせてもらうつもりです。あなたに僕たちのために演奏しに来てほしいです。火，水，金曜日の午後 7 時から午後 9 時まで練習があります。僕たちはスプリングフィールド公民館の 208 号室で練習しています。あなたの最も都合のいい日はいつですか。3 人全員が僕たちのために演奏してくれた後で，1 人を誘います。ホームページで僕たちの音楽を聞くことができます。アドレスは www.springfieldfive.com です。
ダン

送信者：メラニー・ジョーンズ
受信者：ダン・キャンベル
日付：10 月 1 日
件名：すばらしい音楽

ダンさんへ
あなたたちの音楽はすばらしいと思います。水曜日にそちらへ行きたいです。私は『メイビー・トゥモロー』という歌を練習しています。私が自分で書いた歌です。気に入っていただけるとうれしいです。あなたとバンドの他のメンバーの皆さんとお会いできることにわくわくしています。
メラニー

⇒別冊 p.20 ～ 21

解答と解説

解答

(1) ④　(2) ①　(3) ③　(4) ③　(5) ②

解説

(1) 第 1 段落第 3・4 文の内容から考えて，**4** が正解。

設問・選択肢の和訳

(1) アニー・ロンドンデリーの計画は何だったか。
× 1 新しい種類の自転車を作ること。
× 2 家族との休暇を取ること。
× 3 他の国の人々にボストンのことを教えること。
○ 4 世界中を旅すること。

(2) 第 2 段落第 5・7 文の内容から考えて，**1** が正解。

設問・選択肢の和訳

(2) ロンドンデリーがシカゴを出発した後，…
○ 1 彼女はより速く自転車で走ることができた
× 2 彼女は体重が 20 キログラム減った
× 3 彼女は旅をやめた
× 4 彼女はボストンへ行った

(3) 第 3 段落第 7・8 文の内容から考えて，**3** が正解。

設問・選択肢の和訳

(3) ロンドンデリーは…によってお金を得た
× 1 フランスで人々から盗むこと。
× 2 自分の自転車のタイヤを売ること。
○ 3 自転車に案内板をつけること。
× 4 香水などの品を運ぶこと。

(4) 旅を終えた後のロンドンデリーについては第 4 段落に記述があり，第 3 文に She also told many stories about her trip とあるので，**3** が正解。

設問・選択肢の和訳

(4) ロンドンデリーの旅が終わった後，…
× 1 彼女は再び中国へ行った。
× 2 彼女は自分が殺したトラを人々に見せた。
○ 3 彼女は旅についていくつかの話をした。
× 4 彼女は多くのお金を譲(ゆず)った。

(5) 第4段落の最後の文に she showed people that women could do anything that men could do とあるので，**2** が正解。

設問・選択肢の和訳

(5) ロンドンデリーは人々に…ということを示した
× 1 アメリカの自転車が最高だ。
◯ 2 女性は男性と同じことをすることができる。
× 3 重い自転車の方が軽い自転車よりも優れている。
× 4 アジアのトラは危険である。

語句

DOWN LOAD

〈第 1 段落〉

- □ A named B　Bという名前のA
- □ say goodbye to ～　～に別れを告げる
- □ ride a bicycle　自転車に乗る
- □ return　(動) 戻(もど)る

〈第 2 段落〉

- □ at first　最初(のうち)は
- □ heavy　(形) 重い
- □ each　(副) ～につき
- □ think about ～　～について考える
- □ light　(形) 軽い

〈第 3 段落〉

- □ take a boat　船に乗る
- □ stole ＜ steal　(動) ～を盗む
- □ finally　(副) ついに，しまいには
- □ hurt　(動) ～をけがする，傷つける
- □ foot　(名) 足
- □ ask O to *do*　Oに～するよう頼む
- □ company　(名) 会社
- □ sign　(名) 表示，掲示，案内板
- □ show　(動) 表示する，示す
- □ tire　(名) タイヤ
- □ perfume　(名) 香水

〈第 4 段落〉

- □ travel across　横断する
- □ fought ＜ fight　(動) 戦う
- □ tiger　(名) トラ
- □ around the world　世界中
- □ in those days　当時は
- □ weak　(形) 弱い
- □ anything　(名) (肯定文で) 何でも

〈設問・選択肢〉

- □ give away　～を譲る，手放す
- □ dangerous　(形) 危険な

Unit 11

構造確認 ※誤読した部分の確認に使用してください。

⇒別冊 p.20 ～ 21

第1段落 1894年6月，アニー・ロンドンデリーは自転車で世界一周の旅を始めた。

① (In June 1894), an American woman 〈named Annie Londonderry〉 started a long trip. 注1

S V O

(1894年6月)，〈アニー・ロンドンデリーという名の〉アメリカ人女性が長い旅を始めた。

② She said goodbye (to her husband and children 〈in Boston〉) and started [riding her bicycle].

S V① O① V② O②

彼女は (〈ボストンの〉夫と子供たちに) 別れを告げ，[自転車に乗り] 始めた。

③ Her plan was [to ride it (all around North America, Europe, and Asia), and return (to Boston)]. 注2

S V C

彼女の計画は [それ (自転車) に乗って (北アメリカ，ヨーロッパ，アジアの全域を回り)，(ボストンに) 戻ること] だった。

④ It was a round-the-world trip!

S V C

それは世界一周の旅だった！

第2段落 最初は自転車が重く，あまり乗れなかったが，軽い自転車を手に入れてスピードアップした。

① (At first), Londonderry rode a very heavy bicycle.

S V O

(最初のうちは)，ロンドンデリーはとても重い自転車に乗っていた。

② It was more than 20 kilograms. 注3

S V C

それは20キログラムを超える重さだった。

③ She could (only) ride about 12 to 15 kilometers (each day).
S V O

彼女は (1日につき) 約12～15キロメートル (しか) 乗れなかった。

④ She thought (about [ending her trip]).
S V

彼女は ([旅をやめること] を) 考えた。

⑤ But (then) (in Chicago), she got a lighter bicycle.
S V O

しかし (その後) (シカゴで)，彼女はもっと軽い自転車を手に入れた。

⑥ It was (only) 10 kilograms.
S V C

それは (わずか) 10キログラムだった。

⑦ (After that), she could ride much faster.
S V

(その後)，彼女はずっと速く乗れた。

第3段落 フランスでは多くの問題からお金が必要になり，会社の宣伝をする代わりにお金をもらった。

① Londonderry took a boat (from New York to France).
S V O

ロンドンデリーは (ニューヨークからフランスまで) 船に乗った。

② She had many problems (in France).
S V O

(フランスでは) 多くの問題があった。

③ (First), someone stole her money.
S V O

(まず)，何者かが彼女のお金を盗んだ。

④ The weather was (also) very bad.
S V C

天候 (も) 非常に悪かった。

⑤ (Finally), she hurt her foot.
S V O

(しまいには)，彼女は足をけがした。

⑥ She needed more money.
S V O

彼女はより多くのお金を必要とした。

⑦ She asked companies to pay her (to put their names on signs) (on her bicycle). 注4
S V O

彼女は (いくつかの) 会社に (自分の自転車の) (案内板にそれらの会社の名前を載せることで) 代金を払ってもらえるよう頼んだ。

⑧ She showed things 〈like bicycle tires and perfume〉. 注5
S V O

彼女は〈自転車のタイヤや香水などの〉製品を表示した。

第4段落 彼女は世界中を回るという偉業を成しとげ，女性も男性と同じことができると人々に示した。

① Londonderry traveled (across Europe and Asia), and she returned (to Chicago) (in 1895).
S① V① S② V②

ロンドンデリーは (ヨーロッパとアジアを) 横断し，(1895 年に) (シカゴに) 戻った。

② She became famous and got a lot of money.
S V① C① V② O②

彼女は有名になり，大金を得た。

③ She (also) told many stories 〈about her trip〉.
S V O

彼女は〈自分の旅について〉多くの話 (も) した。

④ She fought (in a war) (in China) and killed tigers (in Asia).
S V① V② O②

彼女は (中国では) (争いの中で) 戦い (アジアでは) トラを殺した。

⑤ Many 〈of her stories〉 were not true, but she (still) did a great thing.
S① V① C① S② V② O②

〈彼女の話の〉多くは真実ではなかったが，(それでも) 彼女は偉業を成しとげた。

⑥ She traveled (around the world).
S V

彼女は (世界中を) 旅した。

⑦ (In those days), many people thought [women were weaker than men].
S V O S' V' C'

注6

(当時)，多くの人々が [女性は男性より弱い] と考えていた。

⑧ But she showed people [that women could do anything 〈that men could do〉].
S V O O S' V' O'

注7

しかし彼女は [〈男性ができる〉ことは何でも女性はできるということ] を人々に示した。

注1　A named B は「B という名前の A」という意味です。named は過去分詞で，「…される」「…された」という意味で，直前の名詞を修飾することができます。

注2　この文での to 不定詞は「…すること」という意味で，名詞の働きをしています。

注3　more than ～は「～よりも多い」という意味です。more は much や many の比較級です。

注4　ask 人 to V は「人に V するように頼む」という意味になります。

注5　この文での like は前置詞で，「～のような」「～のように」という意味になります。

注6　weak のような短めの形容詞に -er の語尾をつけると比較級となります。長めの形容詞の場合には直前に more を置きます。「～よりも」という意味で，比較する相手を表す場合には than ～を使います。

注7　that という関係代名詞から後ろの部分が anything という名詞を修飾しています。この that は省略することもできます。

Unit 11

サイトトランスレーション

⇒別冊 p.20 ~ 21

1 In June 1894, /	1894年6月,
an American woman /	あるアメリカ人女性が
named Annie Londonderry /	アニー・ロンドンデリーという名の
started /	始めた
a long trip. //	長い旅を。
She said /	彼女は告げた
goodbye /	別れを
to her husband and children /	夫と子供たちに
in Boston /	ボストンの
and started riding /	そして乗って出発した
her bicycle. //	自転車に。
Her plan was /	彼女の計画は…だった
to ride it /	それに乗って
all around North America, Europe, and Asia, /	北アメリカ, ヨーロッパ, アジアの全域を回り,
and return to Boston. //	そしてボストンに戻る。
It was a round-the-world trip! //	それは世界一周の旅だった!
2 At first, /	最初,
Londonderry rode /	ロンドンデリーは乗っていた
a very heavy bicycle. //	とても重い自転車に。
It was /	それは…だった
more than 20 kilograms. //	20キログラムを超える(重さ)。

She could only ride /	彼女は乗るだけだった
about 12 to 15 kilometers /	約 12 ～ 15 キロメートル
each day. //	1 日につき。
She thought /	彼女は考えた
about ending /	終わらせることについて
her trip. //	彼女の旅を。
But then /	しかしその後
in Chicago, /	シカゴで,
she got /	彼女は手に入れた
a lighter bicycle. //	もっと軽い自転車を。
It was only 10 kilograms. //	それはわずか 10 キログラムだった。
After that, /	その後,
she could ride /	彼女は乗れた
much faster. //	ずっと速く。
3 Londonderry took a boat /	ロンドンデリーは船に乗った
from New York to France. //	ニューヨークからフランスまで。
She had many problems /	彼女には多くの問題があった
in France. //	フランスでは。
First, /	まず,
someone stole her money. //	何者かが彼女のお金を盗んだ。
The weather was also very bad. //	天候も非常に悪かった。
Finally, /	しまいには,
she hurt her foot. //	彼女は足をけがした。
She needed /	彼女は必要とした

more money. //	より多くのお金を。
She asked /	彼女は頼んだ
companies /	いくつかの会社に
to pay her /	彼女にお金を支払ってもらうように
to put their names /	それらの会社の名前を載せることで
on signs /	案内板に
on her bicycle. //	彼女の自転車の。
She showed things /	彼女は製品を表示した
like bicycle tires and perfume. //	自転車のタイヤや香水のような。
4 Londonderry traveled /	ロンドンデリーは進んで行った
across Europe and Asia, /	ヨーロッパとアジアを渡って,
and she returned /	そして彼女は戻った
to Chicago /	シカゴに
in 1895. //	1895 年に。
She became famous /	彼女は有名になった
and got /	そして得た
a lot of money. //	大金を。
She also told /	また彼女は話した
many stories /	多くの話を
about her trip. //	旅行について。
She fought /	彼女は戦った
in a war /	争いの中で
in China /	中国の
and killed tigers /	そしてトラを殺した

in Asia. //	アジアでは。
Many of her stories were not true, /	彼女の話の多くは真実ではなかった,
but she still did /	しかし彼女はそれでも成しとげた
a great thing. //	偉業を。
She traveled /	彼女は旅したのだ
around the world. //	世界中を。
In those days, /	当時,
many people thought /	多くの人々が考えていた
women were weaker than men. //	女性は男性より弱いと。
But she showed /	しかし彼女は示した
people /	人々に
that women could do /	女性ができるということを
anything /	何でも
that men could do. //	男性ができることを。

問題英文と全訳

⇒別冊 p.20 ~ 21

Annie Londonderry

In June 1894, an American woman named Annie Londonderry started a long trip. She said goodbye to her husband and children in Boston and started riding her bicycle. Her plan was to ride it all around North America, Europe, and Asia, and return to Boston. It was a round-the-world trip!

At first, Londonderry rode a very heavy bicycle. It was more than 20 kilograms. She could only ride about 12 to 15 kilometers each day. She thought about ending her trip. But then in Chicago, she got a lighter bicycle. It was only 10 kilograms. After that, She could ride much faster.

Londonderry took a boat from New York to France. She had many problems in France. First, someone stole her money. The weather was also very bad. Finally, she hurt her foot. She needed more money. She asked companies to pay her to put their names on signs on her bicycle. She showed things like bicycle tires and perfume.

Londonderry traveled across Europe and Asia, and she returned to Chicago in 1895. She became famous and got a lot of money. She also told many stories about her trip. She fought in a war in China and killed tigers in Asia. Many of her stories were not true, but she still did a great thing. She traveled around the world. In those days, many people thought women were weaker than men. But she showed people that women could do anything that men could do.

アニー・ロンドンデリー

1894年6月，アニー・ロンドンデリーという名のアメリカ人女性が長い旅を始めた。彼女はボストンの夫と子供たちに別れを告げ，自転車に乗り始めた。彼女の計画は，北アメリカ，ヨーロッパ，アジアの全域を自転車で回り，ボストンに戻ることだった。それは世界一周の旅だった！

最初のうちは，ロンドンデリーはとても重い自転車に乗っていた。それは20キログラムを超える重さだった。彼女は1日につき約12～15キロメートルしか乗れなかった。彼女は旅をやめようかと考えた。しかしその後シカゴで，もっと軽い自転車を手に入れた。それはわずか10キログラムだった。その後，彼女はずっと速く乗ることができた。

ロンドンデリーは，ニューヨークからフランスまで船に乗った。フランスでは多くの問題があった。まず，何者かが彼女のお金を盗んだ。天候も非常に悪かった。しまいには足にけがをした。彼女はより多くのお金を必要とした。彼女は（いくつかの）会社に頼んで，自分の自転車につけた案内板にその会社の名前を載せ，その代金を払ってもらった。彼女は自転車のタイヤや香水などの製品を表示した。

ロンドンデリーはヨーロッパとアジアを横断し，1895年にシカゴに戻った。彼女は有名になり，大金を得た。彼女は旅行についての多くの話もした。彼女は中国では争いの中で戦い，アジアではトラを殺した。話の多くは真実ではなかったが，それでも彼女は偉業を成しとげたのだ。世界中を旅したのだから。当時，多くの人々が女性は男性より弱いと考えていた。しかし，彼女は男性ができることなら何でも女性にもできるということを人々に示したのである。

⇒別冊 p.22 ~ 23

解答と解説

解答

(1) ④　(2) ①　(3) ②　(4) ②　(5) ②

解説

(1) 第1段落第2・3・4文の内容から考えて，**4** が正解。

設問・選択肢の和訳

(1) 浴槽(よくそう)レースはなぜ始まったのか。

×1 新しい船用モーターを検査するため。

×2 新しいタイプの浴槽を売るため。

×3 浴槽で海を渡ろうとするため。

○4 カナダの誕生日を祝うため。

---

(2) 第2段落第4文に Only 47 of them[=bathtubs] finished the race.（それらのうち 47 槽だけがレースを完走した。）とあるので，**1** が正解。

設問・選択肢の和訳

(2) 最初のレースではいくつの船がゴールしたか。

○1 47。

×2 57。

×3 100。

×4 200。

---

(3) 第3段落第2文の後半に he[=Frank Ney] was also the city's mayor（彼はまたその市の市長だった）とあるので，**2** が正解。

設問・選択肢の和訳

(3) フランク・ネイは…だった

×1 有名な海賊(かいぞく)。

○2 ナナイモ市長。

×3 レースが大好きな観光客。

×4 船の製作者。

---

(4) 第4段落第2・3・4文の内容から考えて，**2** が正解。

設問・選択肢の和訳

(4) 1970 年代に，…

×1 レースはより長くなった。

○2 浴槽はより速くなった。

×3 レースはオーストラリアへ移転した。

×4 浴槽のサイズが大きくなった。

(5) すべての段落に race という語が出てくることから考えて，**2** が正解。

設問・選択肢の和訳

(5) この話は…についてのものである
×1 浴槽の歴史。
○2 ゆかいなタイプのレース。
×3 ラスティ・ハリソンの人生。
×4 新しい種類のモーター。

語句

DOWN LOAD

〈タイトル〉

□ bathtub	(名) 浴槽
□ race	(名) レース，競走

〈第 1 段落〉

□ decide	(動) ～を決める，決定する
□ hold	(動) ～を催す
□ celebrate	(動) ～を祝う
□ funny	(形) ゆかいな
□ kind	(名) 種類
□ motor	(名) モーター
□ International World Championship	国際世界選手権

〈第 2 段落〉

□ around	(副) 約，およそ
□ island	(名) 島
□ rescue	(動) ～を救助する
□ winner	(名) 優勝者，勝利者

〈第 3 段落〉

□ dress like ～	～のような服装をする
□ have fun	楽しむ
□ tourist	(名) 観光客

〈第 4 段落〉

□ made of ～	～でできた，～製の
□ first place	1 位，首位
□ just	(副) ほんの，わずかに

〈設問・選択肢〉

□ test	(動) ～を検査する

構造確認 ※誤読した部分の確認に使用してください。

⇒別冊 p.22 ~ 23

第 1 段落 1967 年，ナナイモはカナダ建国 100 周年を祝福するため，浴槽世界選手権レースを始めた。

① Nanaimo is a small city 〈near Vancouver (in Canada)〉.
S V C

ナナイモは〈(カナダの) バンクーバー近くの〉小都市である。

② (In 1967), Canada was 100 years old.
S V C

(1967 年)，カナダは建国 100 周年だった。

③ People 〈in Nanaimo〉 decided to hold a special event (to celebrate Canada's birthday).
S V O

注1

〈ナナイモの〉人々は (カナダの誕生日を祝福するために) 特別な行事を開くことを決めた。

④ They made a funny kind of race.
S V O

彼らはゆかいなタイプのレースを作った。

⑤ They asked people to put motors on bathtubs and see [who could go the fastest (in them)].
S V O V'

注2

彼らは人々に浴槽にモーターをつけて [(それに乗って) 誰が最速で進めるか] を確かめるよう求めた。

⑥ It was called the Great International World Championship Bathtub Race.
S V C

それは大浴槽国際世界選手権レースと呼ばれた。

第 2 段落 最初のレースには約 200 の浴槽が参加したが，それらは重く，47 槽しか完走できなかった。

① There were around 200 bathtubs (in the first race).
V S

(最初のレースには) 約 200 の浴槽が参加した。

② Nanaimo is (on an island), and the bathtubs had to go (about 58 kilometers) (across the sea) (to the city 〈of Vancouver〉).

S① V① S② V②

ナナイモは（島に）あり，浴槽は（海を渡って）（都市〈バンクーバー〉まで）（約58キロメートル）進まなければならなかった。

③ Bathtubs are heavy and they are not made (to go (in the sea)).

S① V① C① S② V②

浴槽は重く，((海上を) 進むためには) 作られていない。

④ Only 47 〈of them〉 finished the race.

S V O

〈それらのうち〉47槽だけがレースを完走した。

⑤ The others needed to be rescued (by people 〈in boats〉). 注3

S V

その他は（〈船に乗った〉人々に）救出される必要があった。

⑥ The first winner was a man 〈named Rusty Harrison〉.

S V C

最初の勝者は〈ラスティ・ハリソンという名の〉男性だった。

第3段落 最も有名なレーサーの1人フランク・ネイは一度もレースに勝たなかったが大いに楽しんだ。

① One 〈of the most famous racers〉 was a man 〈named Frank Ney〉.

S V C

〈最も有名なレーサーの〉1人は〈フランク・ネイという名の〉男性だった。

② He helped to start the first race (in Nanaimo), and he was (also) the city's mayor. 注4

S① V① O① S② V② C②

彼は（ナナイモで）最初のレースを始めるのを手伝い，（また）その市の市長だった。

③ He loved boats, and he (often) dressed (like a pirate) (when he was racing).

S① V① O① S② V② S' V'

彼は船が大好きで，(レースをするときは) (しばしば) (海賊のような) 服を着た。

④ He (never) won, but he had a lot of fun.

S① V① S② V② O②

彼は (一度も) 勝た (なかった)，しかし大いに楽しんだ。

⑤ He (also) liked the race (because it brought many tourists (to Nanaimo)).

S V O S' V' O'

彼は (また) (それが (ナナイモに) 多くの観光客を連れてくるから) そのレースが好きだった。

第４段落 レースに使われる浴槽はガラス繊維（せんい）製に変わりモーターも大きくなり，スピードも上がった。

① The bathtubs 〈used (in the first race)〉 were real bathtubs. 注5

S V C

〈(最初のレースで) 使われた〉浴槽は本当の浴槽だった。

② But (in the 1970s), some Australian people started [coming (to Nanaimo for the race)].

S V O

しかし (1970 年代に)，オーストラリア人の中には [(そのレースのためにナナイモに) 来] 始めた人もいた。

③ They used bathtubs 〈made (of fiberglass)〉.

S V O

彼らは〈(ガラス繊維) 製の〉浴槽を使った。

④ They were lighter, so they were faster.

S① V① C① S② V② C②

それらはより軽かった，そのため (スピードも) より速かった。

⑤ People (also) started [using bigger motors].

S V O

人々は (また) [より大きなモーターを使い] 始めた。

⑥ (In 1967), the first place finisher won the race (in three hours and 26 minutes).
S V O

(1967 年には)，1 着は (3 時間 26 分で) レースに勝った。

⑦ (In 2016), the best time was (just) one hour and seven minutes.
S V C

(2016 年には)，最高記録は (わずか) 1 時間 7 分だった。

注1 decide to V は「V すると決める」という意味です。2 つ目の to 不定詞は「V するために」という意味で目的を表しています。

注2 ask 人 to V は「人に V するように頼む，求める」という意味です。who から them までの部分は，「誰が…するか」という意味の名詞のカタマリを作っています。このように疑問詞の後ろに動詞や SV が続き，名詞のカタマリを作ることがあります。

注3 need to V は「V する必要がある」という意味で，to の後ろには be rescued という受動態の表現が続いています。受動態の後ろで動作の主を表すには，by という前置詞が使われます。

注4 help (to) V は「V するのを助ける」「V するのに役立つ」という意味の表現です。to が略されて，help の後ろに原形動詞が続くこともあります。

注5 used から race までの部分は，直前の The bathtubs という名詞を修飾しています。このように，過去分詞は「…される」「…された」という意味で直前の名詞を修飾することができます。

Unit 12

サイトトランスレーション

⇒別冊 p.22 ~ 23

1 Nanaimo is a small city /	ナナイモは小都市である
near Vancouver /	バンクーバー近くの
in Canada. //	カナダの。
In 1967, /	1967 年,
Canada was 100 years old. //	カナダは建国 100 周年だった。
People in Nanaimo decided /	ナナイモの人々は決めた
to hold a special event /	特別な行事を開くことを
to celebrate /	祝福するために
Canada's birthday. //	カナダの誕生日を。
They made /	彼らは作った
a funny kind of race. //	ゆかいなタイプのレースを。
They asked	彼らは求めた
people /	人々に
to put motors /	モーターをつけることを
on bathtubs /	浴槽に
and see /	そして見ることを
who could go the fastest /	誰が最速で進めるかを
in them. //	それに乗って。
It was called /	それは呼ばれた
the Great International World Championship Bathtub Race. //	大浴槽国際世界選手権レースと。
2 There were around 200 bathtubs /	約 200 の浴槽があった（参加した）

in the first race. //	最初のレースには。
Nanaimo is on an island, /	ナナイモは島の上にあり,
and the bathtubs had to go /	浴槽は進まなければならなかった
about 58 kilometers /	約 58 キロメートル
across the sea /	海を渡って
to the city of Vancouver. //	都市バンクーバーまで。
Bathtubs are heavy, /	浴槽は重い,
and they are not made /	そしてそれらは作られていない
to go in the sea. //	海上を進むために。
Only 47 of them finished /	それらのうち 47 槽だけが終えた
the race. //	レースを。
The others needed /	その他は必要だった
to be rescued /	救出されることが
by people /	人々によって
in boats. //	船に乗った。
The first winner /	最初の勝者は
was a man /	男性だった
named Rusty Harrison. //	ラスティ・ハリソンという名の。
3 One of the most famous racers /	最も有名なレーサーの 1 人は
was a man /	男性だった
named Frank Ney. //	フランク・ネイという名の。
He helped /	彼は手伝った
to start the first race /	最初のレースを始めることを
in Nanaimo, /	ナナイモで,

and he was also the city's mayor. //	そして彼はまたその市の市長だった。
He loved /	彼は大好きだった
boats, /	船が,
and he often dressed /	そして彼はしばしば服を着た
like a pirate /	海賊のような
when he was racing. //	レースをするときは。
He never won, /	彼は一度も勝たなかった,
but he had a lot of fun. //	しかし大いに楽しんだ。
He also liked /	彼はまた好んだ
the race /	そのレースを
because it brought many tourists /	それが多くの観光客を連れてくるから
to Nanaimo. //	ナナイモに。
4 The bathtubs /	浴槽は
used in the first race /	最初のレースで使われた
were real bathtubs. //	本当の浴槽だった。
But in the 1970s, /	しかし 1970 年代に,
some Australian people started coming /	オーストラリア人の中には来るようになった人もいた
to Nanaimo /	ナナイモに
for the race. //	そのレースのために。
They used /	彼らは使った
bathtubs /	浴槽を
made of fiberglass. //	ガラス繊維製の。
They were lighter, /	それらはより軽く,
so they were faster. //	ゆえにより速かった。

People also started using /	人々は使うようにもなった
bigger motors. //	より大きなモーターを。
In 1967, /	1967 年には,
the first place finisher won the race /	1 着（の選手）はそのレースを勝った
in three hours and 26 minutes. //	3 時間 26 分で。
In 2016, /	2016 年には,
the best time /	最高記録は
was just one hour and seven minutes. //	わずか 1 時間 7 分だった。

⇒別冊 p.22 ~ 23

The Bathtub Race

Nanaimo is a small city near Vancouver in Canada. In 1967, Canada was 100 years old. People in Nanaimo decided to hold a special event to celebrate Canada's birthday. They made a funny kind of race. They asked people to put motors on bathtubs and see who could go the fastest in them. It was called the Great International World Championship Bathtub Race.

There were around 200 bathtubs in the first race. Nanaimo is on an island, and the bathtubs had to go about 58 kilometers across the sea to the city of Vancouver. Bathtubs are heavy, and they are not made to go in the sea. Only 47 of them finished the race. The others needed to be rescued by people in boats. The first winner was a man named Rusty Harrison.

One of the most famous racers was a man named Frank Ney. He helped to start the first race in Nanaimo, and he was also the city's mayor. He loved boats, and he often dressed like a pirate when he was racing. He never won, but he had a lot of fun. He also liked the race because it brought many tourists to Nanaimo.

The bathtubs used in the first race were real bathtubs. But in the 1970s, some Australian people started coming to Nanaimo for the race. They used bathtubs made of fiberglass. They were lighter, so they were faster. People also started using bigger motors. In 1967, the first place finisher won the race in three hours and 26 minutes. In 2016, the best time was just one hour and seven minutes.

浴槽レース

ナナイモはカナダのバンクーバー近くの小都市である。1967年，カナダは建国100周年だった。ナナイモの人々はカナダの誕生日を祝福するために特別な行事を開くことに決めた。ゆかいなタイプのレースを作ったのだ。主催者は人々に対して，浴槽にモーターをつけて，それに乗って誰が最速で進めるかを確かめるように求めた。それは大浴槽国際世界選手権レースと呼ばれた。

最初のレースには約200の浴槽が参加した。ナナイモは島にあり，浴槽は海を渡って都市バンクーバーまで約58キロメートル進まねばならなかった。浴槽は重く，海上を進むように作られてはいない。それらのうち47槽しかレースを完走できなかった。その他は船に乗った人々に救出される必要があった。最初の勝者はラスティ・ハリソンという名の男性だった。

最も有名なレーサーの1人は，フランク・ネイという名の男性だった。彼はナナイモの最初のレースを始める手伝いをし，その市の市長でもあった。彼は船が大好きで，レースをするときはしばしば海賊のような服を着た。彼は一度も勝たなかったが，大いに楽しんだ。多くの観光客がレースを見にナナイモに来たことも，彼がそのレースを好きな理由だった。

最初のレースで使われた浴槽は本当の浴槽だった。しかし1970年代に，オーストラリア人たちがレースに参加するためにナナイモに来るようになった。彼らはガラス繊維製の浴槽を使った。そちらの方が軽かったので，スピードも速かった。人々はより大きなモーターを使うようにもなった。1967年には，1着は3時間26分で優勝した。2016年の最高記録は，わずか1時間7分だった。

⇒別冊 p.24 ~ 25

解答と解説

解答

(1) ③　(2) ②　(3) ③　(4) ①　(5) ④

解説

(1) 第 1 段落の最後の文に He ran away very quickly. とあり，He はその前の文から Bobbie であることがわかるので，**3** が正解。

設問・選択肢の和訳

(1) ブレイザー一家のインディアナ州への旅行中に，何が起きたか。
×1 ブレイザー一家は運転中に道に迷った。
×2 ブレイザー一家は新しい 3 匹の犬を手に入れた。
○3 ボビーが逃げた。
×4 ボビーはブレイザー一家の親戚(しんせき)を気に入らなかった。

(2) 第 2 段落の最後の 2 文の内容から考えて，**2** が正解。

設問・選択肢の和訳

(2) 1924 年 2 月に何が起きたか。
×1 ボビーがウォルコットの人々によって発見された。
○2 ボビーがブレイザー一家のカフェに入ってきた。
×3 ブレイザー一家は新聞に広告を載せた。
×4 ブレイザー一家は新しい白黒の犬を手に入れた。

(3) 第 3 段落第 4 文の In Portland, he stayed with a woman who gave him food and put bandages on his legs. から考えて，**3** が正解。

設問・選択肢の和訳

(3) 誰かがボビーの脚に包帯を巻いたのはどこだったか。
×1 ウォルコット。
×2 シルバートン。
○3 ポートランド。
×4 インディアナ州。

(4) 第 4 段落第 3・4 文の内容から考えて，**1** が正解。

設問・選択肢の和訳

(4) ボビーが家に帰った後で，何が起きたか。
○1 ボビーは映画に出た。
×2 ボビーはアメリカ中を旅した。
×3 ブレイザー一家は彼に関する本を書いた。
×4 ブレイザー一家は病気になった。

(5) 全体の内容から，ボビーが遠くから自宅に帰って来たことが本文の主題だとわかるので，**4** が正解。

設問・選択肢の和訳

(5) この話は…についてのものである
×1 有名なカフェ。
×2 犬のためのレース。
×3 多くの犬を飼っていた家族。
○4 とても遠くに旅した犬。

語句

DOWN LOAD

〈第 1 段落〉

□ go on vacation	休暇に出かける
□ terrible	(形) 恐ろしい，怖い
□ attack	(動) ～を攻撃する
□ run away	逃げる，走り去る

〈第 2 段落〉

□ ask O for ～	O に～を求める
□ even	(副) ～ (で) さえ
□ go home	帰宅する
□ without	(前) ～なしに
□ later	(副) ～後に
□ own	(動) ～を所有する

〈第 3 段落〉

□ all the way	はるばる
□ swam < swim	(動) 泳ぐ
□ wide	(形) 広い
□ on the way	途中で
□ accident	(名) 事故，災難
□ hurt *one*'s leg badly	脚に大けがをする
□ stay with ～	～の家に泊まる
□ thin	(形) やせている
□ steak	(名) ステーキ
□ welcome O home	O の帰宅を歓迎する

〈第 4 段落〉

□ all over ～	～中で
□ play	(動) ～を演じる，出演する
□ oneself	(代) 自分自身を
□ die	(動) 死ぬ
□ hundreds of ～	何百の～
□ say goodbye to ～	～に別れを告げる

〈設問・選択肢〉

□ get lost	道に迷う
□ come home	帰宅する
□ race	(名) レース，競走
□ far	(副) 遠くに，遠くへ

Unit 13

構造確認

※誤読した部分の確認に使用してください。

⇒別冊 p.24 ～ 25

第 1 段落 ブレイザー一家は休暇に出かけたが，連れて行った飼い犬ボビーが他の犬に攻撃され逃げた。

① (In August 1923), the Brazier family went on vacation.
S: the Brazier family / V: went

(1923 年 8 月)，ブレイザー一家は休暇に出かけた。

② They lived (in Silverton, Oregon), but they drove (to Wolcott, Indiana), (to visit their relatives).
S①: They / V①: lived / S②: they / V②: drove

注1

彼らは (オレゴン州，シルバートンに) 住んでいたが，(親戚を訪問するために)，(インディアナ州，ウォルコットへ) 車で行った。

③ Oregon is (on the west side 〈of America〉), but Indiana is (on the east side).
S①: Oregon / V①: is / S②: Indiana / V②: is

オレゴン州は (〈アメリカの〉西部に) あるが，インディアナ州は (東部に) ある。

④ Silverton is about 4,100 kilometers (from Wolcott).
S: Silverton / V: is / C: about 4,100 kilometers

シルバートンは (ウォルコットから) 約 4,100 キロメートルある。

⑤ The family took their dog, Bobbie, but something terrible happened.
S①: The family / V①: took / O①: their dog, Bobbie / S②: something terrible / V②: happened

一家は彼らの飼い犬，ボビーを連れて行ったが，恐ろしいことが起こった。

⑥ Bobbie was attacked (by three other dogs).
S: Bobbie / V: was attacked

ボビーは (他の 3 頭の犬に) 攻撃された。

⑦ He ran away (very quickly).
S: He / V: ran

彼は (とてもすばやく) 逃げた。

第２段落 一家はボビーを様々な方法で探したが見つからなかった。しかし，６か月後に戻ってきた。

① The Braziers drove (all around Wolcott).
S V

ブレイザー一家は（ウォルコット中を）車で回った。

② They asked people (for information 〈about their big brown and white dog〉).
S V O

注3

彼らは人々に（《彼らの茶色と白色の大きな犬についての》情報を）求めた。

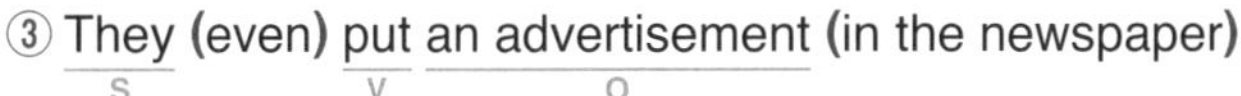

③ They (even) put an advertisement (in the newspaper).
S V O

彼らは（新聞に）広告（まで）出した。

④ But no one saw Bobbie.

S V O

注4

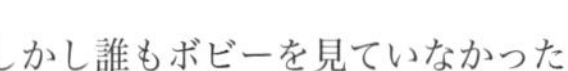

しかし誰もボビーを見ていなかった。

⑤ (After a few days), they had to go (home) (without Bobbie).
S V

（数日後），彼らは（ボビー抜きで）（家に）帰らなければならなかった。

⑥ (Six months later), (in February 1924), the Brazier family was (in the café 〈that they owned〉).
S V

（6か月後の），（1924年２月），ブレイザー一家は（《彼らが所有する》カフェに）いた。

⑦ They were very surprised (because Bobbie walked (into the café)).
S V C S' V'

（ボビーが（カフェの中に）歩いてきたので）彼らは非常に驚いた。

第３段落 ボビーは4,100kmを旅して帰ってきた。一家は彼の帰宅を歓迎するためパーティーを開いた。

① Bobbie came (all the way) (from Wolcott to Silverton).
S V

ボビーは（ウォルコットからシルバートンまで）（はるばる）やってきた。

② He swam (across wide rivers) and walked (through snowstorms).
S V① V②

彼は泳いで（広い川を渡り），（吹雪の中を）歩いた。

③ (On the way), Bobbie had an accident and hurt his legs (badly).
S V① O① V② O②

（途中で），ボビーは事故にあって脚を（ひどく）けがした。

④ (In Portland), he stayed (with a woman 〈who gave him food and put bandages (on his legs)〉). 注5
S V V'① O'① O'① V'② O'②

（ポートランドでは），彼は（〈えさをくれて（脚に）包帯を巻いてくれた〉女性のところに）泊まった。

⑤ He traveled 4,100 kilometers, and he was very thin.
S① V① O① S② V② C②

彼は 4,100 キロメートルを旅して，とてもやせていた。

⑥ The Braziers gave him a big steak and had a party (to welcome him home).
S V① O① O① V② O②

ブレイザー一家は彼に大きなステーキを食べさせ，（彼の帰宅を歓迎するために）パーティーを開いた。

第４段落 ボビーは新聞記事になり，全米で有名になった。後に映画化されたときは自らの役を演じた。

① (In 1924), the Silverton newspaper wrote a story 〈about Bobbie's trip〉.
S V O

（1924 年に），シルバートン新聞は〈ボビーの旅に関する〉記事を書いた。

② Other newspapers saw the story, and Bobbie became famous (all over America).
S① V① O① S② V② C②

他の新聞（社）がその記事を見て，ボビーは（アメリカ中で）有名になった。

③ A book was written (about Bobbie), and (then) a movie was made (about him), (too).
S① V① S② V②

(ボビーについて) 本が書かれ，(その後) (彼について) 映画 (も) 作られた。

④ Bobbie played himself (in it)!
S V O

ボビーは (その中で) 自らを演じた！

⑤ (When Bobbie got sick and died (in 1927)), hundreds of people came (to say goodbye to him).
S' V'① C'① V'② S V

注6

((1927 年に) ボビーが病気になって死んだとき), (彼に別れを告げるために) 何百人もの人々がやって来た。

注1 この文での to 不定詞は「…するために」という意味で，運転して向かった目的を表すために使われています。

注2 something や nothing などを修飾する場合，形容詞はこれらの直後につけます。something terrible で「何か恐ろしいこと」という意味です。

注3 ask A for B は「A に B を求める」という意味です。for という前置詞には「～するために」という意味に加えて，「～を求めて」という意味があります。

注4 no one を主語にした文は，「誰も…ない」という意味の否定文になります。

注5 who は関係代名詞で，who ... legs の部分は a woman という名詞を修飾しています。英語では，このように修飾部分が日本語と逆になり，後ろにくるので注意しましょう。

注6 この文での when は接続詞として使われています。when S V で「S が V するとき」という意味になります。

Unit 13

サイトトランスレーション

⇒別冊 p.24 ~ 25

1 In August 1923, /	1923年8月に,
the Brazier family went /	ブレイザー一家は出かけた
on vacation. //	休暇に。
They lived /	彼らは住んでいた
in Silverton, /	シルバートンに,
Oregon, /	オレゴン州の,
but they drove /	しかし彼らは車で行った
to Wolcott, /	ウォルコットへ,
Indiana, /	インディアナ州の,
to visit their relatives. //	親戚を訪問するために。
Oregon is on the west side /	オレゴン州は西部にある
of America, /	アメリカの,
but Indiana is /	しかしインディアナ州は…にある
on the east side. //	東部に。
Silverton is about 4,100 kilometers /	シルバートンは約4,100キロメートル離れている
from Wolcott. //	ウォルコットから。
The family took /	一家は連れて行った
their dog, /	飼い犬を,
Bobbie, /	ボビーという,
but something terrible happened. //	しかし恐ろしいことが起こった。
Bobbie was attacked /	ボビーは攻撃された

by three other dogs. //	他の３頭の犬に。
He ran away /	ボビーは逃げた
very quickly. //	とてもすばやく。
2 The Braziers drove /	ブレイザー一家は車で回った
all around Wolcott. //	ウォルコット中を。
They asked people /	彼らは人々に求めた
for information /	情報を
about their big brown and white dog. //	彼らの茶色と白色の大きな犬について。
They even put an advertisement /	彼らは広告まで出した
in the newspaper. //	新聞に。
But no one saw /	しかし誰も見ていなかった
Bobbie. //	ボビーを。
After a few days, /	数日後,
they had to go home /	彼らは帰宅しなければならなかった
without Bobbie. //	ボビー抜きで。
Six months later, /	6か月後,
in February 1924, /	1924年２月に,
the Brazier family was in the café /	ブレイザー一家はカフェにいた
that they owned. //	彼らが所有する。
They were very surprised /	彼らは非常に驚いた
because Bobbie walked /	ボビーが歩いてきたので
into the café. //	カフェの中に。
3 Bobbie came /	ボビーはやって来た
all the way /	はるばる

from Wolcott to Silverton. //	ウォルコットからシルバートンまで。
He swam /	彼は泳いだ
across wide rivers /	広い川を渡り
and walked through snowstorms. //	そして吹雪の中を歩いた。
On the way, /	途中で，
Bobbie had an accident /	ボビーは事故にあった
and hurt his legs /	そして足にけがをした
badly. //	ひどく。
In Portland, /	ポートランドでは，
he stayed /	彼は泊まった
with a woman /	ある女性の家に
who gave him food /	彼にえさをくれて
and put bandages /	包帯を巻いてくれた
on his legs. //	彼の脚に。
He traveled /	彼は旅した
4,100 kilometers, /	4,100 キロメートルを，
and he was very thin. //	そしてとてもやせていた。
The Braziers gave him /	ブレイザー一家は彼に与えた
a big steak /	大きなステーキを
and had a party /	そしてパーティーを開いた
to welcome him home. //	彼の帰宅を歓迎するために。
4 In 1924, /	1924 年，
the Silverton newspaper wrote a story /	シルバートン新聞は記事を書いた
about Bobbie's trip. //	ボビーの旅に関する。

Other newspapers saw /	他の新聞も見た
the story, /	その記事を，
and Bobbie became famous /	そしてボビーは有名になった
all over America. //	アメリカ中で。
A book was written /	本が書かれた
about Bobbie, /	ボビーについて，
and then /	そしてその後
a movie was made /	映画が作られた
about him, too. //	彼に関して，また。
Bobbie played /	ボビーは演じた
himself /	彼自身を
in it! //	その中で！
When Bobbie got sick and died /	ボビーが病気になって死んだとき
in 1927, /	1927 年に，
hundreds of people /	何百人もの人々が
came to say goodbye to him. //	彼に別れを告げるためにやって来た。

問題英文と全訳

⇒別冊 p.24 ~ 25

Bobbie the Wonder Dog

In August 1923, the Brazier family went on vacation. They lived in Silverton, Oregon, but they drove to Wolcott, Indiana, to visit their relatives. Oregon is on the west side of America, but Indiana is on the east side. Silverton is about 4,100 kilometers from Wolcott. The family took their dog, Bobbie, but something terrible happened. Bobbie was attacked by three other dogs. He ran away very quickly.

The Braziers drove all around Wolcott. They asked people for information about their big brown and white dog. They even put an advertisement in the newspaper. But no one saw Bobbie. After a few days, they had to go home without Bobbie. Six months later, in February 1924, the Brazier family was in the café that they owned. They were very surprised because Bobbie walked into the café.

Bobbie came all the way from Wolcott to Silverton. He swam across wide rivers and walked through snowstorms. On the way, Bobbie had an accident and hurt his legs badly. In Portland, he stayed with a woman who gave him food and put bandages on his legs. He traveled 4,100 kilometers, and he was very thin. The Braziers gave him a big steak and had a party to welcome him home.

In 1924, the Silverton newspaper wrote a story about Bobbie's trip. Other newspapers saw the story, and Bobbie became famous all over America. A book was written about Bobbie, and then a movie was made about him, too. Bobbie played himself in it! When Bobbie got sick and died in 1927, hundreds of people came to say goodbye to him.

超犬ボビー

1923年8月，ブレイザー一家は休暇に出かけた。彼らはオレゴン州シルバートンに住んでいたが，親戚を訪問するためにインディアナ州ウォルコットへ車で行った。オレゴン州はアメリカ西部にあるが，インディアナ州は東部にある。シルバートンはウォルコットから約4,100キロメートル離れている。一家は飼い犬のボビーを連れて行ったが，恐ろしいことが起こった。ボビーは他の3頭の犬に攻撃された。ボビーはとてもすばやく逃げた。

ブレイザー一家はウォルコット中を車で回った。彼らは人々に，茶色と白色の大きな犬についての情報を求めた。新聞広告まで出した。しかし，誰もボビーを見ていなかった。数日後，彼らはボビー抜きで帰宅しなければならなかった。6か月後の1924年2月，ブレイザー一家は彼らが所有するカフェにいた。ボビーがカフェの中に歩いてきたので，彼らは非常に驚いた。

ボビーは，ウォルコットからシルバートンまではるばるやってきた。彼は広い川を泳いで渡り，吹雪の中を歩いた。途中でボビーは事故にあい，脚に大けがをした。ポートランドではある女性の家に泊まり，その女性はえさをくれて脚に包帯を巻いてくれた。彼は4,100キロメートルを旅して，とてもやせていた。ブレイザー一家は彼に大きなステーキを食べさせ，彼の帰宅を歓迎するためにパーティーを開いた。

1924年，シルバートン新聞はボビーの旅に関する記事を書いた。他の新聞社もその記事を見て，ボビーはアメリカ中で有名になった。ボビーについて本が書かれ，その後，彼について映画も作られた。ボビーはその中で自らを演じた！　1927年にボビーが病気になって死んだとき，彼に別れを告げるために何百人もの人々がやって来た。

Unit 14

⇒別冊 p.26 ～ 27

解答と解説

解答

(1) ④　(2) ③　(3) ③　(4) ③　(5) ②

解説

(1) 第 1 段落の最後の 2 文の内容から考えて，**4** が正解。

設問・選択肢の和訳

(1) ブルジュ・アル・アラブは…であると人々は言う
× 1　世界最大のホテル。
× 2　ドバイの他のホテルよりも安い。
× 3　ガイドブックに載っていないホテル。
○ 4　7 つ星ホテル。

(2) 第 2 段落の第 6 文に It was finally completed in 1999. とあるので，**3** が正解。

設問・選択肢の和訳

(2) ブルジュ・アル・アラブが完成したのはいつか。
× 1　1994 年。
× 2　1997 年。
○ 3　1999 年。
× 4　2000 年。

(3) 第 3 段落第 2・3 文の内容から考えて，**3** が正解。

設問・選択肢の和訳

(3) ブルジュ・アル・アラブの大半の客は…
× 1　無料のスーツケースをもらえる。
× 2　高速列車に乗ることができる。
○ 3　高価な車でそこに到着する。
× 4　他のホテルで入浴する。

(4) 第 4 段落第 1・2 文の内容から考えて，**3** が正解。

設問・選択肢の和訳

(4) ブルジュ・アル・アラブの客は特別な気分を感じる，なぜなら…からだ
× 1　無料の iPad を家に持って帰れる。
× 2　プレゼントとして金をもらえる。
○ 3　多くの異なるものから選べる。
× 4　枕(まくら)の中に金がある。

(5) 文章全体がブルジュ・アル・アラブという豪華(ごうか)ホテルの説明だから，**2** が正解。

設問・選択肢の和訳

(5) この話は…についてのものである
× 1 新しい種類の船。
○ 2 高価なホテル。
× 3 ドバイの空港。
× 4 ホテルで働く人々。

語句

DOWN LOAD

〈第1段落〉

- □ rich (形) 豊かな
- □ guidebook (名) ガイドブック
- □ cheap (形) 安い，安価な
- □ simple (形) 簡素な
- □ enough (形) 十分な，不足のない

〈第2段落〉

- □ island (名) 島
- □ ocean (名) 海
- □ work on ～ ～に取り組む
- □ finally (副) ついに，とうとう
- □ look like ～ ～のように見える
- □ sail (名) 帆(ほ)

〈第3段落〉

- □ take a bus or train バスか電車を利用する
- □ most of ～ ～の大部分
- □ pick up ～ ～を車で迎えに行く
- □ take O out of ～ O を～から取り出す
- □ clothes (名) 服
- □ get O ready O を準備する

〈第4段落〉

- □ cost (動) (お金が) かかる
- □ stay (動) 滞在(たいざい)する
- □ choice (名) 選択肢
- □ for example たとえば
- □ menu (名) メニュー，一覧表
- □ borrow (動) ～を借りる
- □ made of ～ ～でできている，～製の

構造確認 ※誤読した部分の確認に使用してください。

⇒別冊 p.26 ~ 27

第1段落 ブルジュ・アル・アラブはドバイで最も豪華なホテルであり，7つ星とも言われている。

① Dubai(S) is(V①) one(C①) 〈of the world's richest cities〉 and has(V②) many expensive hotels(O②).

ドバイは〈世界で最も豊かな都市の〉1つであり，多くの高価なホテルがある。

② The most luxurious one(S) is(V) the Burj Al Arab(C).

最も豪華なホテルがブルジュ・アル・アラブである。

③ Many guidebooks(S) give(V) stars(O) (to hotels).

多くのガイドブックが（ホテルに）星を与える。

④ A cheap, simple hotel(S①) gets(V①) (just) one star(O①), and the best hotels(S②) 〈in the world〉 get(V②) five stars(O②).

安く，簡素なホテルは星を1つ（だけ）もらい，〈世界で〉最高のホテルは星を5つもらう。

⑤ But some people(S) say(V) [that(S') is(V') not enough(C') (for the Burj Al Arab)](O).

しかし［（ブルジュ・アル・アラブには）それでは不十分だ］と言う人もいる。

⑥ They(S) say(V) [it(S') should get(V') seven stars(O')](O).

［それ（ブルジュ・アル・アラブ）は7つ星をもらうべきだ］と彼らは言う。

第2段落 その建設は1994年に始まり，2,000を超える人々が毎日作業に従事し，1999年に完成した。

① Workers(S) started(V) [building the Burj Al Arab](O) (in 1994).

作業員たちは（1994年に）［ブルジュ・アル・アラブの建設］を始めた。

② (First), they built an island (in the ocean).
S V O

(最初に), 彼らは (海に) 島を築いた。

③ It took three years. 

S V O

それが3年かかった。

④ (Then), work 〈on the hotel building〉 started (in 1997).
S V

(それから), 〈ホテルの建設〉作業が (1997年に) 始まった。

⑤ More than 2,000 people worked (on it) (every day).
S V

2,000人を超える人々が (毎日) (それ (作業) に) 従事した。

⑥ It was (finally) completed (in 1999).
S V

それは (1999年) (ついに) 完成した。

⑦ Many people say [the building is beautiful (because it looks like the sail 〈of a boat〉)].
S V O S' V' C'

多くの人々が [その建物は (〈船の〉帆のように見えるので) 美しい] と言う。

第3段落 その客のほとんどは空港で高級車に迎えられ, 部屋には執事がいて24時間いつでも呼べる。

① (When guests go (to hotels) (from the airport)), they (usually) take a bus or train.
S' V' S V O

(客は (空港から) (ホテルに) 行くとき), (たいてい) バスや列車に乗る。

② However, most 〈of the Burj Al Arab's guests〉 are picked up (in a Rolls Royce). 注3

しかし，〈ブルジュ・アル・アラブの客の〉大半は（ロールスロイス（という車）に）迎えられる。

③ A Rolls Royce is one 〈of the most expensive cars (in the world)〉.

ロールスロイス（という車）は〈（世界で）最も高価な車の〉1 つである。

④ (When guests arrive (at their room)), there is a butler.

（客が（部屋に）着くと），執事がいる。

⑤ This is a person 〈who does everything (for the guests)〉.

この人（執事）は〈（客に）何でもしてくれる〉人である。

⑥ The butler (even) takes their clothes (out of the suitcase) and gets a bath ready (for them).

執事は（スーツケースから）服を取り出して（彼ら（客）のために）風呂の用意（まで）する。

⑦ Guests can call the butler (24 hours a day).

客は執事を（1 日 24 時間（いつでも））呼ぶことができる。

第 4 段落 多額の料金がかかるが，客は特別な気分を感じられるよう，多くの選択肢を与えられる。

① The hotel costs a lot of money, and it wants its guests to feel special (when they stay (there)). 注4

そのホテルは多額の料金がかかるが，客には（彼らが（そこに）滞在する間）特別な気分を感じてほしいと考えている。

② Guests are given many choices.
S V O

客はたくさんの選択肢を与えられる。

③ (For example), there is a menu 〈with 17 different kinds of pillows 〈for guests to choose from〉〉.
V S

(たとえば), 〈〈客が選べる〉17 の異なる種類の枕の〉メニューがある。

④ Also, there is gold (on the walls and the chairs), and guests can borrow an iPad 〈made of gold〉.
V① S① S② V② O②

また, (壁といすには) 金が (使って) あり, 客は〈金で作られた〉iPad を借りることができる。

注1 one of the 最上級 ~s は「最も~な中の一つ」という意味の, よく使われる表現です。

注2 「時間がかかる」という意味を表現する場合には, it takes 時間 という形にします。「お金がかかる」場合は, it costs お金 という形になります。

注3 however は, 前後の意味を「しかしながら」という意味でつなぐ副詞です。直前に述べられている内容に反することを述べる前に使われます。

注4 want 人 to V は「人に V してほしい」という意味の表現です。

Unit 14

サイトトランスレーション

⇒別冊 p.26 ~ 27

1 Dubai is one of the world's richest cities /	ドバイは世界で最も豊かな都市の１つである
and has many expensive hotels. //	そして多くの高価なホテルがある。
The most luxurious one /	最も豪華なホテルが
is the Burj Al Arab. //	ブルジュ・アル・アラブである。
Many guidebooks give /	多くのガイドブックが与える
stars /	星を
to hotels. //	ホテルに。
A cheap, simple hotel gets /	安くて，簡素なホテルはもらう
just one star, /	星を１つだけ，
and the best hotels /	そして最高のホテルは
in the world /	世界で
get five stars. //	星を５つもらう。
But some people say /	しかし言う人々もいる
that is not enough /	それは十分ではないと
for the Burj Al Arab. //	ブルジュ・アル・アラブには。
They say /	彼らは言う
it should get /	そのホテルはもらうべきだと
seven stars. //	７つ星を。
2 Workers started building /	作業員たちは建設し始めた
the Burj Al Arab /	ブルジュ・アル・アラブを
in 1994. //	1994 年に。

First, /	最初に,
they built /	彼らは築いた
an island /	島を
in the ocean. //	海に。
It took three years. //	それは３年かかった。
Then, /	それから,
work on the hotel building started /	ホテルの建設作業が始まった
in 1997. //	1997 年に。
More than 2,000 people worked on it /	2,000 人を超える人々がその作業に従事した
every day. //	毎日。
It was finally completed /	それはついに完成した
in 1999. //	1999 年に。
Many people say /	多くの人々は言う
the building is beautiful /	建物が美しいと
because it looks like the sail /	それが帆のように見えるので
of a boat. //	船の。
3 When guests go /	客が行くとき
to hotels /	ホテルに
from the airport, /	空港から,
they usually take /	彼らはたいてい乗る
a bus or train. //	バスや列車に。
However, /	しかし,
most of the Burj Al Arab's guests /	ブルジュ・アル・アラブの客の大半は
are picked up /	迎えられる

in a Rolls Royce. //	ロールスロイス（という車）で。
A Rolls Royce is one of the most expensive cars /	ロールスロイス（という車）は最も高価な車の１つである
in the world. //	世界で。
When guests arrive at their room, /	客が部屋に着くと，
there is a butler. //	執事がいる。
This is a person /	執事は人である
who does everything for the guests. //	客のためにすべてのことをする。
The butler even takes their clothes out /	執事は客の服さえ取り出して
of the suitcase /	スーツケースから
and gets a bath ready /	そして風呂の用意をしてくれる
for them. //	客のために。
Guests can call /	客は呼ぶことができる
the butler /	執事を
24 hours a day. //	１日 24 時間いつでも。
4 The hotel costs /	そのホテルは料金がかかる
a lot of money, /	多額の，
and it wants its guests /	そしてホテルは客に望んでいる
to feel special /	特別な気分を感じることを
when they stay there. //	客がそこに滞在するときは。
Guests are given /	客は与えられる
many choices. //	多くの選択肢を。
For example, /	たとえば，
there is a menu /	メニューがある

with 17 different kinds of pillows /	17の異なる種類の枕の
for guests /	客が
to choose from. //	選ぶことができる。
Also, /	また,
there is gold /	金がある（使われている）
on the walls and the chairs, /	壁といすに,
and guests can borrow /	そして客は借りることができる
an iPad /	iPadを
made of gold. //	金でできた。

⇒別冊 p.26 ~ 27

The Burj Al Arab

Dubai is one of the world's richest cities and has many expensive hotels. The most luxurious one is the Burj Al Arab. Many guidebooks give stars to hotels. A cheap, simple hotel gets just one star, and the best hotels in the world get five stars. But some people say that is not enough for the Burj Al Arab. They say it should get seven stars.

Workers started building the Burj Al Arab in 1994. First, they built an island in the ocean. It took three years. Then, work on the hotel building started in 1997. More than 2,000 people worked on it every day. It was finally completed in 1999. Many people say the building is beautiful because it looks like the sail of a boat.

When guests go to hotels from the airport, they usually take a bus or train. However, most of the Burj Al Arab's guests are picked up in a Rolls Royce. A Rolls Royce is one of the most expensive cars in the world. When guests arrive at their room, there is a butler. This is a person who does everything for the guests. The butler even takes their clothes out of the suitcase and gets a bath ready for them. Guests can call the butler 24 hours a day.

The hotel costs a lot of money, and it wants its guests to feel special when they stay there. Guests are given many choices. For example, there is a menu with 17 different kinds of pillows for guests to choose from. Also, there is gold on the walls and the chairs, and guests can borrow an iPad made of gold.

ブルジュ・アル・アラブ

ドバイは世界で最も豊かな都市の１つであり，多くの高価なホテルがある。最も豪華なホテルがブルジュ・アル・アラブである。多くのガイドブックがホテルに星を与える。安くて簡素なホテルがもらう星は１つだけであり，世界最高のホテルは星を５つもらう。しかし，ブルジュ・アル・アラブにとってそれでは不十分だと言う人もいる。そのホテルは７つ星をもらうべきだと彼らは言う。

作業員たちは1994年にブルジュ・アル・アラブの建設を始めた。最初に彼らは海に島を築いた。それに３年かかった。それから，ホテルの建設作業が1997年に始まった。2,000人を超える人々が毎日作業に従事した。それは1999年ついに完成した。多くの人々は，建物が船の帆のように見えるので美しいと言う。

客は空港からホテルに行くとき，たいていバスや列車に乗る。しかし，ブルジュ・アル・アラブの客のほとんどはロールスロイスで迎えられる。ロールスロイスは世界で最も高価な車の１つである。客が部屋に着くと，執事がいる。執事とは，客に何でもしてくれる人である。執事は客のスーツケースから服を取り出し，客のために風呂の用意までしてくれる。客は執事を１日24時間いつでも呼ぶことができる。

そのホテルは多額の料金がかかるが，客がそこに滞在する間は特別な気分を感じてほしいと考えている。客はたくさんの選択肢を与えられる。たとえば，客は枕を17の異なる種類のメニューの中から選ぶことができる。また，壁といすには金が張られ，客は金でできたiPadを借りることができる。

⇒別冊 p.28 ~ 29

解答と解説

解答

(1) ③　(2) ①　(3) ③　(4) ①　(5) ①

解説

(1) 第1段落第4文に It was 875 kilometers とある。It は第1文中の the Westfield Sydney to Melbourne Ultramarathon を指しているので，**3** が正解。

設問・選択肢の和訳

(1) シドニー－メルボルン間ウルトラマラソンの距離はどのくらいだったか。

× 1 42 キロ。

× 2 61 キロ。

○ 3 875 キロ。

× 4 1983 キロ。

---

(2) 第2段落第1～7文の内容から考えて，**1** が正解。

設問・選択肢の和訳

(2) クリフ・ヤングは他のランナーとどのように違っていたか。

○ 1 彼の方がずっと年上だった。

× 2 彼の方が有名だった。

× 3 彼の方が経験があった。

× 4 彼は体の具合がとても悪かった。

---

(3) 第3段落の最後の2文の内容から考えて，**3** が正解。

設問・選択肢の和訳

(3) ヤングはどのようにしてよいランナーになったか。

× 1 車の後ろを走ってトレーニングした。

× 2 ウマのそばを走った。

○ 3 ヒツジを追いかけた。

× 4 オーストラリア中を旅行した。

---

(4) 第4段落第4文に Young's coach set his alarm clock too early by mistake とあるので，**1** が正解。

設問・選択肢の和訳

(4) ヤングのコーチは何をしたか。

○ 1 ヤングを早く起こしすぎた。

× 2 ヤングにもっと眠るよう言った。

× 3 他のランナーたちと話した。

× 4 間違えて眠り込んだ。

(5) クリフ・ヤングという人物の説明が本文の主題だと考えられるので，**1** が正解。

設問・選択肢の和訳

(5) この話は…についてのものである。

○ 1 有名なランナーになった農民。

× 2 30 人の有名なランナー。

× 3 人とウマとのレース。

× 4 睡眠(すいみん)コンテスト。

語句

DOWN LOAD

〈第 1 段落〉

□ race	(名) レース，競走
□ about	(副) 約，およそ

〈第 2 段落〉

□ farmer	(名) 農民
□ *be* worried that ～	～ということを心配する
□ die	(動) 死ぬ

〈第 3 段落〉

□ sometimes	(副) 時々
□ sheep	(名) ヒツジ
□ farm	(名) 農場，農園
□ practice	(名) 練習

〈第 4 段落〉

□ slow	(形) 遅い
□ coach	(名) コーチ
□ set	(動) セットする，合わせる
□ alarm clock	目覚まし時計
□ by mistake	誤って
□ while	(接) ～する間
□ keep ～ing	～し続ける
□ all over the world	世界中で，世界中に

〈設問・選択肢〉

□ experience	(名) 経験
□ behind	(前) ～の後ろで，～に続いて
□ beside	(前) ～のそばで
□ run after ～	～を追いかける
□ woke < wake	(動) ～を起こす
□ fall asleep	眠り込む

Unit 15

構造確認 ※誤読した部分の確認に使用してください。

⇒別冊 p.28 ~ 29

第 1 段落 シドニー－メルボルン間ウルトラマラソンは長さが 875km で，完走には 6 ~ 7 日かかった。

① (In Australia), there was(V) a famous race(S) 〈called the Westfield Sydney to Melbourne Ultramarathon〉.

(オーストラリアに)，〈ウェストフィールド・シドニー－メルボルン間ウルトラマラソンと呼ばれる〉有名なレースがあった。

② It(S) started(V) (in 1983).

それは (1983 年に) 始まった。

③ A marathon(S①) is(V①) about 42 kilometers long(C①), but this race(S②) was(V②) much longer(C②).

マラソンは約 42 キロメートルの長さだが，このレースはそれよりずっと長かった。

④ It(S①) was(V①) 875 kilometers(C①), and it(S②) took(V②) six or seven days(O②) (to finish).

それは 875 キロメートルあり，(完走するのに) 6 ~ 7 日かかった。

第 2 段落 若くて有名なランナーが多く，61 歳の農民クリフ・ヤングが勝てるとは誰も思わなかった。

① Most of the people(S) 〈in the race〉 were(V) famous runners(C).

〈そのレースの〉人々の大半が有名なランナーだった。

② But one man(S) was(V) different(C).

しかしある男性は違っていた。

③ His name(S) was(V) Cliff Young(C).

彼の名前はクリフ・ヤングだった。

④ He was 61 years old.
S V C

彼は61歳だった。

⑤ He was not a runner.
S V C

彼はランナーではなかった。

⑥ He was a farmer.
S V C

彼は農業をしていた。

⑦ The other runners were under 30.
S V C

他のランナーたちは30歳未満だった。

⑧ No one thought [that Young could win].

S V O S' V'

誰も［ヤングが勝てる］とは思わなかった。

⑨ Some people were worried that he might get sick or die.
S V C S' V'① C'① V'②

彼が病気になったり死んだりするかもしれないと心配する人々もいた。

第3段落 彼は自分の農場で飼っている多くのヒツジを追いかけることが，マラソンの練習になっていた。

① There was something 〈that no one knew (about Young)〉.

V S S' V'

〈(ヤングについて) 誰も知らない〉ことがあった。

② He had a lot of sheep (on his farm).
S V O

彼は (自分の農場で) 多くのヒツジを飼っていた。

③ He was poor, and he did not have a horse or a car.
S① V① C① S② V② O②

彼は貧しく，ウマも車も持っていなかった。

④ He had to chase the sheep.
S V O

彼はヒツジを追いかける必要があった。

⑤ (Sometimes), he chased the sheep (for three days).
S V O

(時々)，彼は (3 日間) ヒツジを追いかけた。

⑥ It was good practice (for the ultramarathon).
S V C

それが (ウルトラマラソンのための) よい練習だった。

第４段落 彼は他のランナーが眠っている間も走り続けて新記録でレースに勝ち，世界で有名になった。

① Young was much slower (than the other runners). 
S V C

ヤングは (他のランナーたちより) ずっと遅かった。

② (After running (for about 18 hours)), the runners stopped (to sleep).
S V

((約 18 時間) 走った後)，ランナーたちは (眠るために) 止まった。

③ They slept (for about six hours).
S V

彼らは (約 6 時間) 眠った。

④ But Young's coach set his alarm clock (too early) (by mistake).
S V O

しかしヤングのコーチは彼の目覚まし時計を (間違えて) (早すぎる時間に) セットしていた。

⑤ Young started running (after sleeping (for two hours)).
S V O

ヤングは((2時間) 眠った後で) 走り始めた。

⑥ (After that), he did not sleep (much).
S V

(その後), 彼は (あまり) 眠らなかった。

⑦ (While the other runners were sleeping), he kept running.
S' V' S V O

(他のランナーたちが眠っている間), 彼は走り続けた。

⑧ He won the race.
S V O

彼はレースに勝った。

⑨ He (also) made a new record 〈of five days, fifteen hours, and four minutes〉.
S V O

彼は〈5日, 15時間, 4分という〉新記録 (も) 作った。

⑩ He became famous (all over the world).
S V C

彼は (世界中で) 有名になった。

注1 A called B は「B と呼ばれる A」という意味の表現です。このように過去分詞は「…される」「…された」という意味で, 直前の名詞を修飾することができます。

注2 「～ (の時間) がかかる」という場合には, it を主語にして it takes 時間 to V という形を使います。

注3 no one を主語にすると「誰も…ない」という意味の否定の文となります。

注4 that ... Young の部分は直前の something という名詞を修飾する関係代名詞節です。that は省略することもできます。

注5 比較級を「ずっと…」という意味で強調する場合には much を使います。than ～は「～よりも」という意味で比較する相手を示します。

注6 while はつなぎ言葉で, while S V という形で「S が V する間」という意味になります。

Unit 15 サイトトランスレーション

DOWN LOAD

⇒別冊 p.28 ~ 29

1 In Australia, /	オーストラリアに,
there was a famous race /	有名なレースがあった
called the Westfield Sydney to Melbourne Ultramarathon. //	ウェストフィールド・シドニー－メルボルン間ウルトラマラソンと呼ばれる。
It started /	それは始まった
in 1983. //	1983 年に。
A marathon is about 42 kilometers long, /	マラソンは約 42 キロメートルの長さである,
but this race was much longer. //	しかしこのレースはそれよりずっと長かった。
It was 875 kilometers, /	それは 875 キロメートルあり,
and it took /	そしてかかった
six or seven days /	6 ~ 7 日
to finish. //	完走するのに。
2 Most of the people /	人々の大半が
in the race /	そのレースの
were famous runners. //	有名なランナーだった。
But one man was different. //	しかしある男性は違っていた。
His name was Cliff Young. //	彼の名前はクリフ・ヤングだった。
He was 61 years old. //	彼は 61 歳だった。
He was not a runner. //	彼はランナーではなかった。
He was a farmer. //	彼は農業をしていた。
The other runners were under 30. //	他のランナーたちは 30 歳未満だった。
No one thought /	誰も思わなかった

that Young could win. //	ヤングが勝てると。
Some people were worried /	心配する人々もいた
that he might get sick or die. //	彼が病気になったり死んだりするかもしれないと。
3 There was something that no one knew /	誰も知らないことがあった
about Young. //	ヤングについて。
He had /	彼は飼っていた
a lot of sheep /	多くのヒツジを
on his farm. //	自分の農場で。
He was poor, /	彼は貧しく,
and he did not have /	そして持っていなかった
a horse or a car. //	ウマも車も。
He had to chase /	彼は追いかけなくてはならなかった
the sheep. //	ヒツジを。
Sometimes, /	時々,
he chased /	彼は追いかけた
the sheep /	ヒツジを
for three days. //	3日間。
It was good practice /	それはよい練習だった
for the ultramarathon. //	ウルトラマラソンのための。
4 Young was much slower /	ヤングはずっと遅かった
than the other runners. //	他のランナーたちより。
After running /	走った後
for about 18 hours, /	約 18 時間,
the runners stopped /	ランナーたちは止まった

to sleep. //	眠るために。
They slept /	彼らは眠った
for about six hours. //	約６時間。
But Young's coach set /	しかしヤングのコーチは合わせた
his alarm clock /	彼の目覚まし時計を
too early /	かなり早く
by mistake. //	間違えて。
Young started running /	ヤングは走り始めた
after sleeping /	眠った後で
for two hours. //	２時間。
After that, /	その後,
he did not sleep much. //	彼はあまり眠らなかった。
While the other runners were sleeping, /	他のランナーたちが眠っている間,
he kept running. //	彼は走り続けた。
He won the race. //	彼はレースに勝った。
He also made /	また彼は作った
a new record /	新記録を
of five days, fifteen hours, and four minutes. //	５日，15 時間，４分という。
He became famous /	彼は有名になった
all over the world. //	世界中で。

Column 「正しい音読」で力をつけよう！

英語の長文が読めるようになるためには，単に問題を解いたり，英文の構造を理解したりするだけではなく，ネイティブの音をまねて音読することが重要です。でも，音読といっても，意味も考えずただ英文を読むのではなく，自分なりに工夫をすることが必要です。

そのような工夫の方法に入る前に，どうして英語の音読が重要なのかを確認してみましょう。4技能試験では，速く英語を読むことがとても大切となります。そのためには，英語を英語のまま，左から右にスラスラと読めるようにならなければなりません。そのための最高の訓練が音読なのです。音読では戻り読みをすることができません。音読しながら意味を理解するためには，止まって日本語に訳すこともできません。もちろん，これは耳で聞いてわかるためにも重要ですから，音読はリスニングの基礎訓練にもなるのです。

音読のような単純作業は，惰性でダラダラとやらないことが重要です。意味を考えずに，ただ繰り返すだけのような音読ではあまり効果はありません。あきないように，さらに効果が上がるように，自分なりに工夫しましょう。たとえば，最初は本書の「サイトトランスレーション」のページを使って，英語と日本語を交互に音読するのもよいでしょう。しかし，日本語に訳しながら読むのはあくまでも通過点にすぎませんから，次は日本語を見ずに，音読しながら意味を理解しましょう。その際，ネイティブの音をまねながらやることを忘れないでください。我流の発音が固まってしまうと，後で直すのに苦労します。その他，オーバーラッピングやシャドウイングなどを組み合わせ，英語のままスラスラわかるようになるまで練習しましょう。

そして，復習については，音声を，ラジオを聞くように定期的に聞いて，内容や語いを忘れないようにキープしましょう。このオーディオプレイヤーを使った復習が，リーディングとリスニングの実力をアップするための鍵です。

⇒別冊 p.28 ~ 29

Cliff Young

In Australia, there was a famous race called the Westfield Sydney to Melbourne Ultramarathon. It started in 1983. A marathon is about 42 kilometers long, but this race was much longer. It was 875 kilometers, and it took six or seven days to finish.

Most of the people in the race were famous runners. But one man was different. His name was Cliff Young. He was 61 years old. He was not a runner. He was a farmer. The other runners were under 30. No one thought that Young could win. Some people were worried that he might get sick or die.

There was something that no one knew about Young. He had a lot of sheep on his farm. He was poor, and he did not have a horse or a car. He had to chase the sheep. Sometimes, he chased the sheep for three days. It was good practice for the ultramarathon.

Young was much slower than the other runners. After running for about 18 hours, the runners stopped to sleep. They slept for about six hours. But Young's coach set his alarm clock too early by mistake. Young started running after sleeping for two hours. After that, he did not sleep much. While the other runners were sleeping, he kept running. He won the race. He also made a new record of five days, fifteen hours, and four minutes. He became famous all over the world.

クリフ・ヤング

オーストラリアに，ウェストフィールド・シドニー－メルボルン間ウルトラマラソンという名の有名なレースがあった。それは1983年に始まった。マラソンは約42キロメートルの長さだが，このレースはそれよりずっと長かった。875キロメートルあり，完走するのに6～7日かかった。

レースに参加する人々の大半が，有名なランナーだった。しかしある男性は違っていた。彼の名前はクリフ・ヤングだった。61歳だった。彼はランナーではなかった。彼は農民だった。他のランナーたちは30歳未満だった。誰もヤングが勝てるとは思わなかった。彼が病気になったり死んだりするかもしれないと心配する人々もいた。

ヤングについて誰も知らないことがあった。彼は自分の農場で多くのヒツジを飼っていた。彼は貧しく，ウマも車も持っていなかった。彼は，ヒツジを追いかける必要があったのである。時々，彼は3日間ヒツジを追いかけた。それはウルトラマラソンのためのよい練習だった。

ヤングは他のランナーたちよりずっと遅かった。約18時間走った後，ランナーたちは眠るために止まった。彼らは約6時間眠った。しかし，ヤングのコーチは間違えて彼の目覚まし時計を早すぎる時間にセットしていた。ヤングは2時間眠った後で走り始めた。その後，彼はあまり眠らなかった。他のランナーたちが眠っている間，彼は走り続けた。彼はレースに勝った。彼は5日と15時間4分という新記録も作った。彼は世界中で有名になった。

⇒別冊 p.30 ～ 31

解答と解説

解答

(1) ② (2) ② (3) ③ (4) ② (5) ③

解説

(1) 第 1 段落の最後の文に It traveled through space and arrived on Mars in August 2012. とある。It は 2 つ前の文中の a robot named Curiosity を指しているので，**2** が正解。

設問・選択肢の和訳

(1) 2012 年 8 月に何が起きたか。
× 1 火星がより寒くなった。
○ 2 あるロボットが火星に到着した。
× 3 科学者たちが火星で生物を見つけた。
× 4 科学者たちが新しい種類のロケットを作った。

(2) 第 2 段落第 2 文の後半に they [=scientists] were worried it [=Curiosity] could break とあるので，**2** が正解。

設問・選択肢の和訳

(2) 科学者たちはなぜ心配したか。
× 1 キュリオシティのパラシュートは小さすぎた。
○ 2 彼らはキュリオシティが壊れるかもしれないと思った。
× 3 キュリオシティのロケットは遅すぎた。
× 4 キュリオシティを運ぶロケットが壊れた。

(3) 第 3 段落の最後の文の後半に Curiosity can study things which are under the ground とあるので，**3** が正解。

設問・選択肢の和訳

(3) キュリオシティは…ことができる
× 1 とても速く動く。
× 2 岩石を地球に持ち帰る。
○ 3 地下のものを見つける。
× 4 長さと幅がより大きくなる。

(4) 第 4 段落の最後の文に Scientists think that Curiosity will be able to travel around Mars for a long time. とあるので，**2** が正解。

設問・選択肢の和訳

(4) 科学者たちは…と考えている
× 1 キュリオシティのコンピュータは故障している。

○2 キュリオシティは長い間利用できる。
×3 キュリオシティは十分な動力を持っていない。
×4 キュリオシティは新しい車輪を必要とする。

(5) どの段落にもキュリオシティという名の火星探査ロボットが出てくるので，**3** が正解。

設問・選択肢の和訳

(5) この話は何についてのものか。
×1 ロケットの歴史。
×2 火星に人類を送ること。
○3 火星で働くロボット。
×4 火星に建物を造ること。

語句

DOWN LOAD

〈タイトル〉

□ curiosity	(名) 好奇心

〈第 1 段落〉

□ human	(名) 人間
□ easily	(副) 容易に，たやすく
□ air	(名) 空気
□ rocket	(名) ロケット
□ robot	(名) ロボット
□ look for ～	～を探す
□ necessary	(形) 必要な
□ support	(動) ～を支える
□ space	(名) 宇宙

〈第 2 段落〉

□ *be* worried	心配する
□ parachute	(名) パラシュート
□ slow ～ down	～の速度を落とす
□ land	(動) 着陸する
□ safely	(副) 安全に，無事に

〈第 3 段落〉

□ wheel	(名) 車輪
□ wide	(形) 幅が～の
□ slowly	(副) ゆっくり，遅く
□ send ～ back	～を送り返す
□ pick up ～	～を拾い上げる
□ rock	(名) 岩石
□ arm	(名) 腕
□ drill	(名) ドリル
□ ground	(名) 地面，地表

〈第 4 段落〉

□ probably	(副) たぶん，おそらく
□ enough	(形) 十分な，不足のない
□ power	(名) エネルギー，動力

Unit 16

構造確認 ※誤読した部分の確認に使用してください。

⇒別冊 p.30 ~ 31

第1段落 キュリオシティ（好奇心）というロボットが，火星を調査するためにロケットで送られた。

① Humans can't live (on Mars) (easily).
S V

人間は（火星で）（簡単には）生きられない。

② There is no air, and it is too cold.
V① S① S② V② C②

空気はないし，寒すぎる。

③ But people want to know (about Mars).
S V

しかし人々は（火星について）知りたいと思っている。

④ (In November 2011), a rocket was sent (to Mars).
S V

（2011年11月に），あるロケットが（火星に）送られた。

⑤ (Inside the rocket) was a robot 〈named Curiosity〉. 
V S

（ロケットの中には）〈キュリオシティ（好奇心）と名づけられた〉ロボットがいた。

⑥ Its job was [to learn about the environment and look for elements 〈necessary to support life〉]. 
S V C

それ（キュリオシティ）の仕事は［環境について学び，〈生命を維持するために必要な〉要素を探すこと］だった。

⑦ It traveled (through space) and arrived (on Mars) (in August 2012).
S V① V②

それは（宇宙を通り抜けて）行き（2012年8月に）（火星に）到着した。

第２段落 キュリオシティは高価なので，科学者たちは壊れることを心配したが，安全に火星に降りた。

① (When Curiosity left the rocket and went down (to Mars) (from space)),
S' V'① V'②

scientists were worried.
S V C

（キュリオシティがロケットから出て（宇宙空間から）（火星に）降りていったとき），科学者たちは心配した。

② Curiosity was expensive, and they were worried it could break.
S① V① C① S② V② C② S' V'

キュリオシティは高価であり，彼らはそれが壊れる可能性があるのを心配していた。

③ Curiosity had to fall down (from the sky).
S V

キュリオシティは（空から）落ちる必要があった。

④ They used a special parachute and small rockets (to slow it down).
S V O

（それの速度を落とすために）彼らは特別なパラシュートと小さなロケットを使った。

⑤ Everyone was happy (when it landed (safely)).

S V C S' V'

（それが（安全に）着陸したとき）全員が喜んだ。

第３段落 キュリオシティは車輪６つ，カメラ 17 台，ドリル付の 2m の腕を持ち，様々なことができる。

① Curiosity has six wheels, and it is 2.9 meters long and 2.7 meters wide.
S① V① O① S② V② C②

キュリオシティは６つの車輪を持ち，それは長さ 2.9 メートルで幅 2.7 メートルである。

② It moves (slowly), but it can do many things.
S① V② S① V② O②

それは（ゆっくり）動くが，多くのことができる。

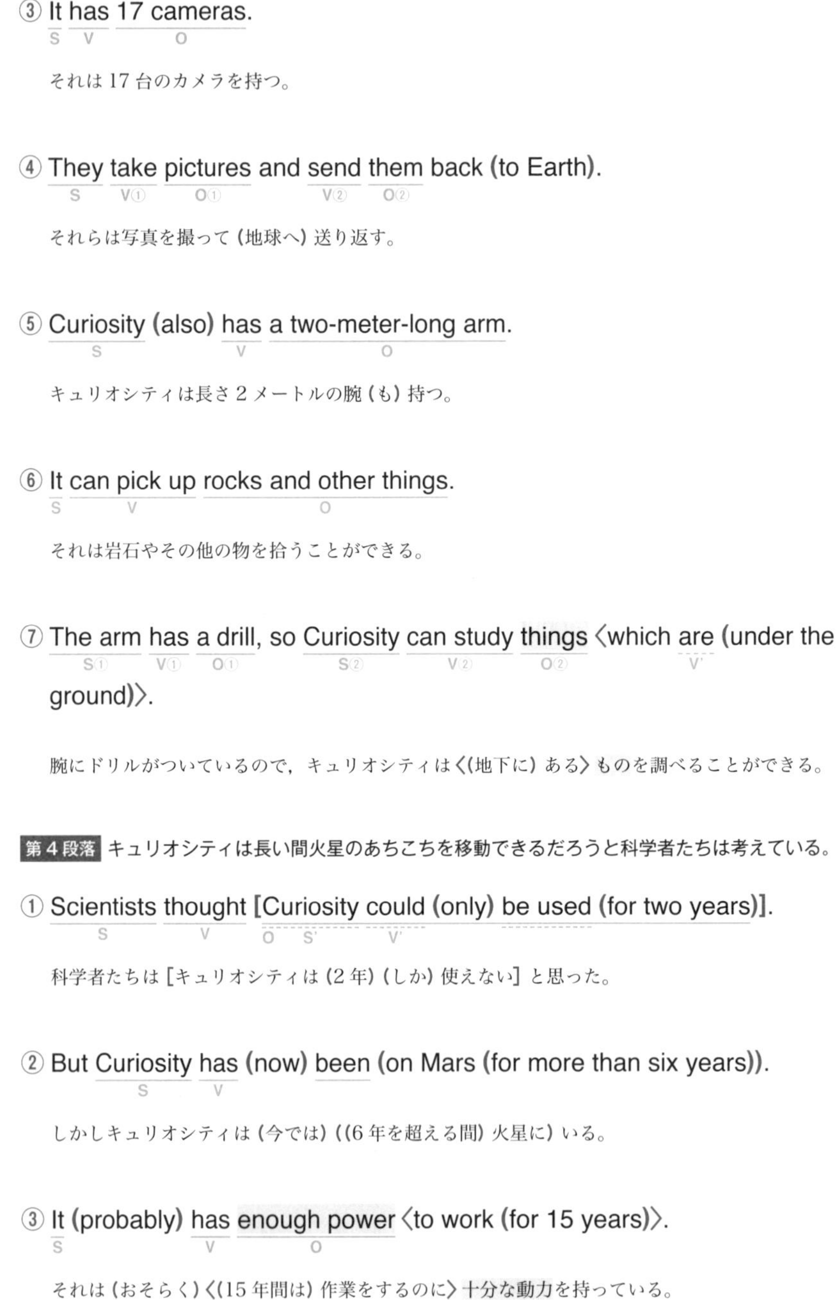

③ It has 17 cameras.
S V O

それは 17 台のカメラを持つ。

④ They take pictures and send them back (to Earth).
S V① O① V② O②

それらは写真を撮って (地球へ) 送り返す。

⑤ Curiosity (also) has a two-meter-long arm.
S V O

キュリオシティは長さ 2 メートルの腕 (も) 持つ。

⑥ It can pick up rocks and other things.
S V O

それは岩石やその他の物を拾うことができる。

⑦ The arm has a drill, so Curiosity can study things 〈which are (under the ground)〉.
S① V① O① S② V② O② V'

腕にドリルがついているので，キュリオシティは〈(地下に) ある〉ものを調べることができる。

第 4 段落 キュリオシティは長い間火星のあちこちを移動できるだろうと科学者たちは考えている。

① Scientists thought [Curiosity could (only) be used (for two years)].
S V O S' V'

科学者たちは [キュリオシティは (2 年) (しか) 使えない] と思った。

② But Curiosity has (now) been (on Mars (for more than six years)).
S V

しかしキュリオシティは (今では) ((6 年を超える間) 火星に) いる。

③ It (probably) has enough power 〈to work (for 15 years)〉.
S V O

それは (おそらく) 〈(15 年間は) 作業をするのに〉十分な動力を持っている。

④ It was (also) built (with many things 〈it might not need〉).
S V S' V'

それには (また) (〈必要ないかもしれない〉多くのものが) 組み込まれていた。

⑤ It has a backup computer (because the main computer may break).
S V O S' V'

それは (メインコンピュータが壊れるかもしれないので) 予備のコンピュータを持っている。

⑥ Also, it does not need all six wheels (to move around).
S V O

また，それは (動き回るのに) 6 つの車輪全部を必要とするわけではない。

⑦ Scientists think [that Curiosity will be able to travel (around Mars) (for a long time)].
S V O S' V'

科学者たちは [キュリオシティは (長い間) (火星のあちこちを) 移動できるだろう] と考えている。

注1 この文は，もともと A robot named Curiosity was inside the rocket. なのですが，下線部の場所を表す句を，強調するために前に出し，動詞と主語を入れ替えることで，文のインパクトを高めています。

注2 to 不定詞は「…すること」という意味で，名詞の働きをするカタマリを作っています。また，necessary という形容詞は，直前の elements という名詞を修飾しています。

注3 この文での when は接続詞です。when S V で「S が V するとき」という意味になります。⑤の文のように，この節が後ろに置かれることもあります。

注4 この文での to 不定詞は「…するために」という意味で，目的を表すために使われています。

注5 it ... need の部分は，直前の many things を修飾しています。thing の後ろに，関係代名詞の that や which が省略されていると考えるとよいでしょう。

Unit 16

サイトトランスレーション

DOWNLOAD

⇒別冊 p.30 ~ 31

1 Humans can't live /	人間は生きられない
on Mars /	火星で
easily. //	容易に。
There is no air, /	空気はなく，
and it is too cold. //	寒すぎる。
But people want to know /	しかし人々は知りたいと思っている
about Mars. //	火星について。
In November 2011, /	2011 年 11 月に，
a rocket was sent /	あるロケットが送られた
to Mars. //	火星に。
Inside the rocket /	ロケットの中には
was a robot /	ロボットがいた
named Curiosity. //	キュリオシティ（好奇心）と名づけられた。
Its job was to learn /	それの仕事は学ぶことだった
about the environment /	環境について
and look for elements necessary /	そして必要な要素を探すこと
to support life. //	生命を支えるための。
It traveled /	それは進んだ
through space /	宇宙を抜けて
and arrived on Mars /	そして火星に着いた
in August 2012. //	2012 年 8 月に。

2 When Curiosity left the rocket /	キュリオシティがロケットを出たとき
and went down /	そして降りた
to Mars /	火星に
from space, /	宇宙空間から,
scientists were worried. //	科学者たちは心配した。
Curiosity was expensive, /	キュリオシティは高価だった,
and they were worried /	彼らは心配した
it could break. //	それが壊れる可能性があるのを。
Curiosity had to fall down /	キュリオシティは落ちる必要があった
from the sky. //	空から。
They used /	彼らは使った
a special parachute and small rockets /	特別なパラシュートと小さなロケットを
to slow it down. //	その速度を落とすために。
Everyone was happy /	全員が喜んだ
when it landed /	キュリオシティが着陸したとき
safely. //	安全に。
3 Curiosity has /	キュリオシティは持つ
six wheels, /	6つの車輪を,
and it is 2.9 meters long /	そしてそれは長さ 2.9 メートルである
and 2.7 meters wide. //	幅 2.7 メートルで。
It moves /	それは動く
slowly, /	ゆっくりと,
but it can do /	しかしすることができる
many things. //	多くのことを。

It has 17 cameras. //	それは 17 台のカメラを持つ。
They take pictures /	それらは写真を撮る
and send them /	そしてそれらを送る
back to Earth. //	地球へ戻して。
Curiosity also has /	またキュリオシティは持つ
a two-meter-long arm. //	長さ２メートルの腕を。
It can pick up /	それは拾うことができる
rocks and other things. //	岩石やその他の物を。
The arm has a drill, /	腕にドリルがついている,
so Curiosity can study /	だからキュリオシティは調べることができる
things which are under the ground. //	地下にあるものを。
4 Scientists thought /	科学者たちは思った
Curiosity could only be used /	キュリオシティは使われるだけだと
for two years. //	２年間。
But Curiosity has now been /	しかしキュリオシティは今ではいる
on Mars /	火星に
for more than six years. //	６年を超える間。
It probably has enough power /	それはおそらく十分な動力を持っている
to work /	作業するのに
for 15 years. //	15 年間。
It was also built /	それにはまた組み込まれた
with many things /	たくさんの物が
it might not need. //	必要ないかもしれない。
It has a backup computer /	それは予備のコンピュータを持っている

because the main computer may break. //	メインコンピュータが壊れるかもしれないから。
Also, /	また,
it does not need /	それは必要としていない
all six wheels /	6つの車輪全部を
to move around. //	動き回るのに。
Scientists think /	科学者たちは考えている
that Curiosity will be able to travel /	キュリオシティは移動できるだろうと
around Mars /	火星のあちこちを
for a long time. //	長い間。

⇒別冊 p.30 ~ 31

Curiosity

Humans can't live on Mars easily. There is no air, and it is too cold. But people want to know about Mars. In November 2011, a rocket was sent to Mars. Inside the rocket was a robot named Curiosity. Its job was to learn about the environment and look for elements necessary to support life. It traveled through space and arrived on Mars in August 2012.

When Curiosity left the rocket and went down to Mars from space, scientists were worried. Curiosity was expensive, and they were worried it could break. Curiosity had to fall down from the sky. They used a special parachute and small rockets to slow it down. Everyone was happy when it landed safely.

Curiosity has six wheels, and it is 2.9 meters long and 2.7 meters wide. It moves slowly, but it can do many things. It has 17 cameras. They take pictures and send them back to Earth. Curiosity also has a two-meter-long arm. It can pick up rocks and other things. The arm has a drill, so Curiosity can study things which are under the ground.

Scientists thought Curiosity could only be used for two years. But Curiosity has now been on Mars for more than six years. It probably has enough power to work for 15 years. It was also built with many things it might not need. It has a backup computer because the main computer may break. Also, it does not need all six wheels to move around. Scientists think that Curiosity will be able to travel around Mars for a long time.

キュリオシティ（好奇心）

人間は火星で簡単には生きられない。空気はないし，寒すぎる。しかし人々は火星について知りたいと思っている。2011 年 11 月に，あるロケットが火星に送られた。ロケットの中には，キュリオシティ（好奇心）と名づけられたロボットがいた。その仕事は環境について学び，生命を維持するために必要な要素を探すことだった。それは宇宙を通り抜けて 2012 年 8 月に火星に到着した。

キュリオシティがロケットから出て宇宙空間から火星に降りたとき，科学者たちは心配した。キュリオシティは高価であり，彼らはそれが壊れる可能性があるのを心配していた。キュリオシティは空から落ちる必要があった。速度を落とすために，彼らは特別なパラシュートと小さなロケットを使った。キュリオシティが安全に着陸したとき，全員が喜んだ。

キュリオシティは 6 つの車輪を持ち，長さ 2.9 メートル，幅 2.7 メートルである。ゆっくり動くが，多くのことができる。17 台のカメラを持つ。それらは写真を撮って地球へ送り返す。キュリオシティはまた長さ 2 メートルの腕も持つ。それは岩石やその他の物を拾うことができる。腕にドリルがついているので，キュリオシティは地下にあるものを調べることができる。

科学者たちは，キュリオシティは 2 年しか使えないと思った。しかし，キュリオシティは今では 6 年を超えて火星にいる。おそらく 15 年間は作業するのに十分な動力を持っている。それには必要ないかもしれない物がたくさん組み込まれてもいた。メインコンピュータが壊れるかもしれないから予備のコンピュータを持っている。また，動き回るのに 6 つの車輪全部が必要なわけではない。キュリオシティは長い間火星のあちこちを移動できるだろうと科学者たちは考えている。

⇒別冊 p.32 ~ 33

解答と解説

解答

(1) ①　(2) ①　(3) ④　(4) ④　(5) ②

解説

(1) 第1段落第1・2文の内容から考えて，**1**が正解。

設問・選択肢の和訳

(1) 1977年，ティエリー・サビーヌは…

○1 砂漠（さばく）で道に迷った。

×2 世界中を旅した。

×3 9,000キロを超えて走った。

×4 新しい種類のバイクを作った。

---

(2) 1978年のダカールラリーについては第2段落第1～6文に記述があり，第6文に Only 74 teams were able to finish the race. とあるので，**1**が正解。

設問・選択肢の和訳

(2) 1978年のダカールラリーでは何チームがゴールしたか。

○1 74チーム。

×2 170チーム。

×3 246チーム。

×4 335チーム。

---

(3) 第3段落第5文に the race went to South America in 2009 とあることから，**4**が正解。

設問・選択肢の和訳

(3) 2009年に，ダカールラリーに何が起きたか。

×1 以前よりずっと長くなった。

×2 より危険になった。

×3 6か国を通り抜け始めた。

○4 南アメリカへ移った。

---

(4) 第4段落第2文の後半の some people say it should be safer から考えて，**4**が正解。

設問・選択肢の和訳

(4) 一部の人々はダカールラリーについて何と言うか。

×1 ヘリコプターが遅すぎる。

×2 異なる車が使用されるべきだ。

×3 医師や看護師がもっと必要だ。

○4 危険すぎる。

(5) どの段落にも race という語が出てくるので，**2** が正解。

設問・選択肢の和訳

(5) この話は…についてのものである
×1 アフリカの都市。
○2 非常に長いレース。
×3 バイクを失った男。
×4 新しい種類のバイク。

語句

DOWN LOAD

〈第 1 段落〉

□ ride a motorcycle	バイクに乗る
□ dangerous	(形) 危険な
□ get lost	道に迷う
□ race	(名) レース，競走
□ want O to be ～	O が～であることを望む

〈第 2 段落〉

□ at the beginning	最初に
□ sand	(名) 砂
□ grass	(名) 草
□ get hurt	けがをする
□ damage	(動) ～に損傷を与える

〈第 3 段落〉

□～ or more	～以上
□ become worried that ～	～ということが心配になる
□ *be* worry about ～	～のことを心配する

〈第 4 段落〉

□ sometimes	(副) 時々，時には
□ die	(動) 死ぬ
□ safe	(形) 安全な，危険のない
□ helicopter	(名) ヘリコプター
□ still	(副) それでもなお

Unit 17

構造確認 ※誤読した部分の確認に使用してください。

⇒別冊 p.32 ~ 33

第 1 段落 ダカールラリーは世界で最も難しいレースで，パリからセネガルまで走らなければならない。

①(In 1977), a French man 〈named Thierry Sabine〉 went (to Libya) (to ride his motorcycle).

S V

(1977 年)，〈ティエリー・サビーヌという名の〉フランス人男性が（リビアへ）行って（バイクに乗った)。

② [Riding (in the desert)] was very dangerous, and he got lost.

S① V① C① S② V② C②

[（砂漠の中を）乗って走ること] は非常に危険であり，彼は道に迷った。

③ But it was (also) beautiful and exciting.

S V C

しかしそれは（また）美しく刺激的であった。

④ He decided to make a new kind of race 〈called the Dakar Rally〉.

S V O

彼は〈ダカールラリーという名の〉新しい種類のレースを作ることに決めた。

⑤ He wanted it to be the world's most difficult race.

S V O

彼はそれを世界で最も難しいレースにしたいと思った。

⑥ The drivers had to travel (from the city 〈of Paris〉 〈in France〉) (to Dakar 〈in the African country〉 〈of Senegal〉).

S V

ドライバーたちは（〈フランスの〉〈パリという〉市から）（〈セネガルという〉〈アフリカの国の〉ダカールまで）進まなければならなかった。

第２段落 最初のレースは1978年に行われ，170チームが参加したが，ゴールしたのは74だけだった。

① The first race was (in 1978).
S V

最初のレースは（1978年に）あった。

② (At the beginning), there were 170 teams (in the race).
V S

（最初），（そのレースには）170チームが（参加して）いた。

③ The drivers did not (usually) drive (on roads).
S V

ドライバーたちは（たいていは）（道路の上を）運転しなかった。

④ They drove (on sand, grass, and gravel).
S V

彼らは（砂，草，砂利の上を）運転した。

⑤ Many 〈of the racers〉 got hurt, and some 〈of their cars and motorcycles〉 were damaged.
S① V① C① S② V②

注3

〈そのレーサー（出場者）の〉多くはけがをし，〈彼らの車やバイクの〉いくつかは壊れた。

⑥ Only 74 teams were able to finish the race.
S V O

74チームだけがレースを終えることができた。

⑦ (In 2018), 335 teams started the race and 246 finished.
S① V① O① S② V②

（2018年には），335チームがレースを始めて246チームが（レースを）終えた。

第３段落 ダカールラリーは何年もの間アフリカで行われてきたが，テロの心配から南米へ移った。

① (For many years), the Dakar Rally was held (in Africa).
S V

（何年もの間），ダカールラリーは（アフリカで）行われた。

② The race was (usually) about 10,000 kilometers long and went (through six or more countries).
S V① C① V②

レースは（通常）約10,000キロの長さで（6か国以上を通り抜けて）行った。

③ But people became worried that Africa was too dangerous.
S V C S' V' C'

しかし人々はアフリカは危険すぎると心配するようになった。

④ They were worried (about terrorism).
S V C

彼らは（テロ行為について）心配した。

⑤ (Because of that), the race went (to South America) (in 2009).
S V

（そのため），レースは（2009年に）（南アメリカへ）移った。

⑥ (This time), it went (through Argentina and Chile).
S V

（この時には），それ（レース）は（アルゼンチンとチリを通って）行った。

第4段落 レースは死傷者が多く，安全性は少しずつ高まってはいるが，それでもやはり危険である。

① People (sometimes) say [that too many racers get hurt (in the Dakar Rally)].
S V O S' V' C'

人々は（時々）[（ダカールラリーでは）けがをするレーサーが多すぎる] と言う。

② More than 70 people have died, and some people say [it should be safer].
S① V① S② V② O②S' V' C'

70を超す人々が死んでいて，[それ（レース）はもっと安全であるべきだ] と言う人もいる。

③ (Now), helicopters watch the racers, and there are many doctors and nurses 〈to help people 〈who get hurt〉〉.

S① V① O① V② S② V' C'

(現在では), ヘリコプターがレーサーたちを見守り, 《〈けがをする〉人々を助けてくれる〉多くの医師と看護師がいる。

④ Also, the cars and motorcycles are becoming safer.

S V C

また, 車やバイクはより安全になってきている。

⑤ But it is (still) a dangerous race.

S V C

しかし (それでも) 危険なレースである。

注1 Riding は動名詞で, この文の主語となっています。このように, 動詞の〜ing 形は名詞のような働きをし, 主語や目的語になることができます。

注2 the city of Paris のように, of がイコールのような働きをし, A of B の形で「B という A」という意味になることもあります。

注3 get ＋過去分詞 は一種の受動態で, 「…される」という意味になります。hurt は, hurt-hurt-hurt と活用する (原形・過去形・過去分詞がすべて同じ形である) ことにも注意しましょう。

注4 because of 〜は「〜のために, 〜のせいで」という意味で原因・理由を表します。直後に, 主語＋動詞 の節が来る場合は because S V となりますが, 名詞や名詞句を一つ, 理由としてくっつけたい場合には because of を使います。

注5 この文での to 不定詞は形容詞のような働きをし, 直前の many doctors and nurses という名詞を修飾しています。また, who は関係代名詞で, who ... hurt の部分は直前の people という名詞を修飾しています。

サイトトランスレーション

DOWNLOAD

⇒別冊 p.32 ~ 33

1 In 1977, /	1977 年,
a French man /	フランス人男性が
named Thierry Sabine /	ティエリー・サビーヌという名の
went to Libya /	リビアへ行って
to ride his motorcycle. //	バイクに乗った。
Riding /	乗って走ることは
in the desert /	砂漠の中を
was very dangerous, /	非常に危険であり,
and he got lost. //	そして彼は道に迷った。
But /	しかし
it was also beautiful and exciting. //	それはまた美しく刺激的であった。
He decided /	彼は決めた
to make /	作ることを
a new kind of race /	新しい種類のレースを
called the Dakar Rally. //	ダカールラリーと呼ばれる。
He wanted it /	彼はそれに望んだ
to be the world's most difficult race. //	世界で最も難しいレースになるように。
The drivers had to travel /	ドライバーたちは進まなければならなかった
from the city of Paris /	パリ市から
in France /	フランスの
to Dakar /	ダカールまで

in the African country of Senegal. //	セネガルというアフリカの国の。
2 The first race was in 1978. //	最初のレースは 1978 年だった。
At the beginning, /	最初は,
there were 170 teams /	170 チームが（参加して）いた
in the race. //	レースに。
The drivers did not usually drive /	ドライバーたちはたいていは運転しなかった
on roads. //	道路の上を。
They drove /	彼らは運転した
on sand, grass, and gravel. //	砂，草，砂利の上を。
Many of the racers got hurt, /	出場者の多くはけがをし,
and some of their cars and motorcycles /	そして彼らの車やバイクのいくつかは
were damaged. //	壊れた。
Only 74 teams were able to finish /	74 チームだけが終えることができた
the race. //	レースを。
In 2018, /	2018 年には,
335 teams started /	335 チームが始めた
the race /	レースを
and 246 finished. //	そして 246 チームがゴールした。
3 For many years, /	何年もの間,
the Dakar Rally was held in Africa. //	ダカールラリーはアフリカで開催された。
The race was usually about 10,000 kilometers long /	レースは通常約 10,000 キロの長さだった
and went through six or more countries. //	そして 6 か国以上を通り抜けた。
But people became worried /	しかし人々は心配するようになった

that Africa was too dangerous. //	アフリカは危険すぎると。
They were worried /	彼らは心配した
about terrorism. //	テロ行為について。
Because of that, /	そのため,
the race went /	レースは移った
to South America /	南アメリカへ
in 2009. //	2009 年に。
This time, /	この時には,
it went through Argentina and Chile. //	それはアルゼンチンとチリを通って行った。
4 People sometimes say /	人々は時々言う
that too many racers get hurt /	けがをするレーサーが多すぎると
in the Dakar Rally. //	ダカールラリーでは。
More than 70 people have died, /	70 を超す人々が死んでいて,
and some people say /	そして言う人々もいる
it should be safer. //	それ（レース）はもっと安全であるべきだと。
Now, /	現在では,
helicopters watch the racers, /	ヘリコプターがレーサーたちを見守り,
and there are many doctors and nurses /	多くの医師と看護師がいる
to help people /	人々を助けてくれる
who get hurt. //	けがをする。
Also, /	また,
the cars and motorcycles are becoming safer. //	車やバイクはより安全になってきている。
But it is still a dangerous race. //	しかしそれでもやはり危険なレースである。

Column 精読に加えて「多読」に挑戦(ちょうせん)しよう！

4技能試験のリーディングの問題では，一つ一つの文をしっかり読む力も大切ですが，同様に，設問に関係ある箇所をすばやく探す力を鍛(きた)えることも重要です。しっかり読む力，すなわち精読力に関しては，本書のような問題集で，読み違えた箇所を確認し，読み違いを減らす努力をしていくとよいでしょう。文法や単語などを学びながら，正確に読む力を鍛えましょう。

そして，設問を先に見て，該当(がいとう)部分を探すような解き方を心がけていれば，該当部分をすばやく探すのもだんだん得意になっていきます。本書や，その他の問題集でたくさん練習しましょう。英検の一つ下の級の過去問をタイムトライアルのような形で数多く解いてみるのも，すばやく英語を処理する力を高めるのに役に立つでしょう。

そのような，試験対策としての長文学習に加えて，私がおすすめしているのが「多読学習」です。多読とは，試験を意識することなく，純粋(じゅんすい)に読書として英語をたくさん読むことです。とはいっても，英語学習者の皆さんが，本場の新聞や雑誌，本などをいきなり読むことは難しいでしょう。だから，ストレスがたまらないレベルで，簡単に書かれた多読用の本から始めるのがよいと思います。

学校や図書館などに多読ライブラリーがないか探してみましょう。そして，そのライブラリーの中からおもしろそうな本を手に取ってみましょう。パラパラとめくって，簡単で，読めそうなレベルだったら，さっそく読み始めてください。もし難しく感じたら，もっと簡単な本を探してみましょう。無理をしないことが肝心(かんじん)です。多読の際には，知らない単語が出てきても，辞書で調べたりせず，想像しながら読んでいきましょう。また，おもしろくないと思ったら，読むのをやめて他の本に移ってもかまいません。あくまでも読書なのだと考えましょう。感想メモなどを日記のように書きためていくこともおすすめです。この多読の習慣を身につけると，英語学習がずっと楽しくなりますよ。

問題英文と全訳

⇒別冊 p.32 ~ 33

The Dakar

In 1977, a French man named Thierry Sabine went to Libya to ride his motorcycle. Riding in the desert was very dangerous, and he got lost. But it was also beautiful and exciting. He decided to make a new kind of race called the Dakar Rally. He wanted it to be the world's most difficult race. The drivers had to travel from the city of Paris in France to Dakar in the African country of Senegal.

The first race was in 1978. At the beginning, there were 170 teams in the race. The drivers did not usually drive on roads. They drove on sand, grass, and gravel. Many of the racers got hurt, and some of their cars and motorcycles were damaged. Only 74 teams were able to finish the race. In 2018, 335 teams started the race and 246 finished.

For many years, the Dakar Rally was held in Africa. The race was usually about 10,000 kilometers long and went through six or more countries. But people became worried that Africa was too dangerous. They were worried about terrorism. Because of that, the race went to South America in 2009. This time, it went through Argentina and Chile.

People sometimes say that too many racers get hurt in the Dakar Rally. More than 70 people have died, and some people say it should be safer. Now, helicopters watch the racers, and there are many doctors and nurses to help people who get hurt. Also, the cars and motorcycles are becoming safer. But it is still a dangerous race.

ザ・ダカール

1977年，ティエリー・サビーヌという名のフランス人男性が，リビアへ行ってバイクに乗った。砂漠の中を乗って走るのは非常に危険であり，彼は道に迷った。しかしそれは，美しく刺激的でもあった。彼は，ダカールラリーという名の新しい種類のレースを作ることに決めた。彼は，それを世界で最も難しいレースにしたいと思った。ドライバーたちは，フランスのパリ市からセネガルというアフリカの国のダカールまで進まなければならなかった。

最初のレースは1978年だった。最初，レースには170チームが参加した。ドライバーたちはたいていは道路の上を走らなかった。彼らは砂，草，砂利の上を走った。出場者の多くはけがをし，彼らの車やバイクのいくつかは壊れた。74チームだけがレースを終えることができた。2018年には，335チームがレースを始めて246チームがゴールした。

何年もの間，ダカールラリーはアフリカで行われた。レースは通常約10,000キロで，6か国以上を通り抜けた。しかし，人々はアフリカが危険すぎると心配するようになった。彼らはテロ行為を心配した。そのため，レースは2009年に南アメリカへ移った。この時には，レースはアルゼンチンとチリを通り抜けた。

人々は時々，ダカールラリーではけがをするレーサーが多すぎると言う。70を超す人々が死んでいて，レースはもっと安全であるべきだと言う人もいる。現在では，ヘリコプターがレーサーたちを見守り，けがをする人々を助けてくれる多くの医師と看護師がいる。また，車やバイクはより安全になってきている。しかしそれでもやはり危険なレースである。

⇒別冊 p.34 ~ 35

解答と解説

解答

(1) ④　(2) ①　(3) ④　(4) ①　(5) ③

解説

(1) 第 1 段落の最後の 2 文の内容から考えて，**4** が正解。

設問・選択肢の和訳

(1) デイビー・クロケットは…のとき家を出た

×1 8歳。

×2 9歳。

×3 12歳。

○4 14歳。

(2) 第 2 段落の最後の 2 文に In one year, Crockett killed 105 of these animals. That made him very famous. とあり，these animals は前の文中の bears を指しているので，**1** が正解。

設問・選択肢の和訳

(2) クロケットは有名になった，なぜなら彼は…からだ

○1 多くのクマを殺した。

×2 新しい種類のロウソクを作った。

×3 自然について人々に教えた。

×4 新しい種類の動物を見つけた。

(3) 第 3 段落の最後の 2 文の内容から考えて，**4** が正解。

設問・選択肢の和訳

(3) 1836 年にクロケットに何が起きたか。

×1 新しい教会を始めた。

×2 メキシコについて人々に教えた。

×3 テキサスに関する本を書いた。

○4 戦いで死んだ。

(4) 第 4 段落に 1950 年代についての記述がある。最後の文に Millions of children wanted to look like Crockett, so they bought these hats. とあり，these hats はその前の第 3 文にある coonskin caps のことを指しているので，**1** が正解。

設問・選択肢の和訳

(4) 1950 年代に，多くの子供たちは…

○1 クーンスキンキャップを買った。

×2 ペットのアライグマを飼っていた。

×3 学校でクロケットについて学んだ。
×4 クロケットに関する本を読んだ。

(5) すべての段落に Crockett という人名が出てくるので，この人物について述べている **3** が正解。

設問・選択肢の和訳

(5) この話は…についてのものである
×1 有名なテレビ番組の俳優。
×2 有名な帽子職人。
○3 多くの冒険をした男性。
×4 メキシコの歴史。

語句

〈第 1 段落〉

□ take ～ on a trip	～を旅に連れて行く，移動させる
□ cow	(名) ウシ
□ leave home	家出する

〈第 2 段落〉

□ forest	(名) 森
□ bear	(名) クマ
□ electricity	(名) 電気
□ candle	(名) ロウソク
□ fat	(名) 脂肪
□ dangerous	(形) 危険な
□ hunt	(動) ～を狩る
□ safety	(名) 安全

〈第 3 段落〉

□ later	(副) 後になって
□ state	(名) 州
□ in those days	当時は
□ help O *do*	O が～するのを手伝う
□ fight	(動) 戦う
□ battle	(名) 戦い
□ church	(名) 教会
□ die	(動) 死ぬ

〈第 4 段落〉

□ TV show	テレビ番組
□ millions of ～	何百万の～
□ look like ～	～のように見える

〈設問・選択肢〉

□ adventure	(名) 冒険

構造確認 ※誤読した部分の確認に使用してください。

⇒別冊 p.34 ~ 35

第1段落 デイビー・クロケットは8歳で銃(じゅう)の撃ち方を学び，14歳のときに学校に行かず家を出た。

① Davy Crockett was born (in the United States in 1786).
S V

デイビー・クロケットは（1786年にアメリカ合衆国で）生まれた。

② His parents had nine children, so it was hard [to get food 〈for everyone〉].
S① V① O① S② V② C②

注1

彼の両親には9人の子供がいたので，[〈全員分の〉食べ物を手に入れるの] は難しかった。

③ He learned [how to shoot a gun] (when he was (just) eight years old) (so he could kill animals (for food)).
S① V① O① S' V' C' S② V② O②

注2

（彼は（わずか）8歳のときに）（(食料のために）動物を殺すことができるように）[銃の撃ち方] を学んだ。

④ (When he was 12), he helped to take cows (on a 600-kilometer trip).
S' V' C' S V O

（彼が12歳のときには），ウシを（600キロ移動）させるのを手伝った。

⑤ (When Crockett was 14), his father wanted him to go to school.
S' V' C' S V O

（クロケットが14歳のとき），彼の父親は彼に学校に行ってほしいと思った。

⑥ Crockett did not like it, so he left home.
S① V① O① S② V② O②

クロケットは学校が好きではなかったので，家出した。

第2段落 彼は森の中が好きで動物についてよく知っていた。1年でクマを105頭殺して有名になった。

① Crockett loved to be (in the forest), and he knew a lot 〈about animals〉.
S① V① S② V② O②

クロケットは（森の中に）いるのが大好きで，〈動物について〉たくさん知っていた。

② (A long time ago), many people ate bear meat.
S V O

(昔), 多くの人はクマの肉を食べた。

③ (Also), people did not have electricity, so they made candles (from bear fat).
S① V① O① S② V② O②

(また), 人々は電気を持っていなかったので, (クマの脂肪から) ロウソクを作っていた。

④ Bears were dangerous animals, but it was important [to hunt them (for food and safety)]. 注3
S① V① C① S② V② C②

クマは危険な動物だったが, [(食料と安全のために) それらを狩ること] は重要だった。

⑤ (In one year), Crockett killed 105 〈of these animals〉.
S V O

(1 年で), クロケットは〈これらの動物の〉105 頭を殺した。

⑥ That made him very famous.
S V O C

そのことは彼を非常に有名にした。

第３段落 当時メキシコの一部だったテキサスへ行った彼は, 自由のための戦いに参加して死んだ。

① (Later), Crockett went (to Texas).
S V

(その後), クロケットは (テキサスへ) 行った。

② (Today), Texas is a state 〈in America〉.
S V C

(今日では), テキサスは〈アメリカの〉州である。

③ But (in those days), Texas was part 〈of Mexico〉.
S V C

しかし (当時), テキサスは〈メキシコの〉一部だった。

④ People 〈in Texas〉 did not like Mexico.
S V O

〈テキサスの〉人々はメキシコが好きではなかった。

⑤ They wanted Texas to be free.
S V O

彼らはテキサスが自由であることを望んだ。

⑥ Crockett went and fought (with them).
S V① V②

クロケットは行って（彼らと一緒に）戦った。

⑦ He was (in a battle 〈at a church 〈called the Alamo〉〉) (in 1836).
S V

彼は（1836 年に）(〈〈アラモという名の〉教会での〉戦いに)（参加して）いた。

⑧ He died, but the battle became famous (because the people were fighting (to be free)).
S① V① S② V② C② S' V'

彼は死んだが，(人々が（自由になるために）戦っていたので）その戦いは有名になった。

第 4 段落 彼に関する TV 番組は世界的に有名になり，番組中で彼が被った帽子を多くの子供が買った。

① (In the 1950s), a TV show was made (about Crockett).
S V

(1950 年代に)，(クロケットに関して）テレビ番組が制作された。

② The show became one 〈of the world's most famous TV shows〉.
S V C

その番組は〈世界で最も有名なテレビ番組の〉1 つになった。

③ (In the show), Crockett wore a special hat 〈called a "coonskin cap"〉.
S V O

(その番組の中で)，クロケットは〈「クーンスキンキャップ」と呼ばれる〉特別な帽子をかぶっていた。

④ It was made (of raccoon fur).
S V

それは（アライグマの毛皮で）作られていた。

⑤ Millions of children wanted to look (like Crockett), so they bought these hats.
S① V① S② V② O②

注4

何百万人の子どもたちが（クロケットのように）見えるようになりたいと思って，帽子を買った。

注1 it は仮主語で，to ... everyone までの部分を指しています。この it は「それ」とは訳しません。

注2 how to V は「どのように V するか」「V する方法」という意味で，名詞のカタマリを作っています。このように，疑問詞＋ to 不定詞 で名詞のカタマリを作ることができます。また，so (that) S can V は「S が V できるように」という意味で，何かをする目的を表すことができます。ここでは，時制の統一のために can の過去形 could が使われています。

注3 it は仮主語で，to 不定詞以下の部分を指しています。この it は「それ」とは訳しません。

注4 so という接続詞は，「だから」「そして」という意味で前後の文をつなぐことができます。

Unit 18

サイトトランスレーション

DOWNLOAD

⇒別冊 p.34 ~ 35

1 Davy Crockett was born /	デイビー・クロケットは生まれた
in the United States /	アメリカ合衆国で
in 1786. //	1786 年に。
His parents had /	両親にはいた
nine children, /	9 人の子供が,
so it was hard /	だから難しかった
to get food /	食べ物を手に入れるのは
for everyone. //	全員分の。
He learned /	彼は学んだ
how to shoot a gun /	銃の撃ち方を
when he was just eight years old /	わずか 8 歳のときに
so he could kill /	殺すことができるように
animals /	動物を
for food. //	食料のために。
When he was 12, /	彼が 12 歳のとき,
he helped to take /	連れて行くのを手伝った
cows /	ウシを
on a 600-kilometer trip. //	600 キロの移動で。
When Crockett was 14, /	クロケットが 14 歳のとき,
his father wanted him to go /	父は彼に行ってほしかった
to school. //	学校に。

Crockett did not like it, /	クロケットは学校が好きではなかった，
so he left home. //	だから家出した。
2 Crockett loved /	クロケットは大好きだった
to be in the forest, /	森の中にいるのが，
and he knew /	そして彼は知っていた
a lot /	たくさん
about animals. //	動物について。
A long time ago, /	昔，
many people ate /	多くの人々が食べた
bear meat. //	クマの肉を。
Also, /	また，
people did not have /	人々は持たなかった
electricity, /	電気を，
so they made /	だから作っていた
candles /	ロウソクを
from bear fat. //	クマの脂肪から。
Bears were dangerous animals, /	クマは危険な動物だった，
but it was important /	しかし重要だった
to hunt them /	クマを狩ることは
for food and safety. //	食料と安全のために。
In one year, /	1 年で，
Crockett killed /	クロケットは殺した
105 of these animals. //	これらの動物の 105 頭を。
That made him very famous. //	それは彼を非常に有名にした。

3 Later, /	その後,
Crockett went /	クロケットは行った
to Texas. //	テキサスへ。
Today, /	今日では,
Texas is a state /	テキサスは州である
in America. //	アメリカの。
But in those days, /	しかしその当時,
Texas was part /	テキサスは一部だった
of Mexico. //	メキシコの。
People /	人々は
in Texas /	テキサスの
did not like /	好きではなかった
Mexico. //	メキシコを。
They wanted /	彼らは望んだ
Texas to be free. //	テキサスに自由であることを。
Crockett went /	クロケットは行った
and fought with them. //	そして彼らと一緒に戦った。
He was in a battle /	彼は戦いに（参加して）いた
at a church /	教会で
called the Alamo /	アラモという名の
in 1836. //	1836 年に。
He died, /	彼は死んだ,
but the battle became famous /	しかしその戦いは有名になった
because the people were fighting /	人々が戦っていたので

to be free. //	自由になるために。
4 In the 1950s, /	1950 年代に,
a TV show was made /	テレビ番組が作られた
about Crockett. //	クロケットに関して。
The show became /	その番組はなった
one of the world's most famous TV shows. //	世界で最も有名なテレビ番組の 1 つに。
In the show, /	番組の中で,
Crockett wore /	クロケットは身につけていた（かぶっていた）
a special hat /	特別な帽子を
called a "coonskin cap." //	「クーンスキンキャップ」と呼ばれる。
It was made /	それは作られていた
of raccoon fur. //	アライグマの毛皮で。
Millions of children wanted to look /	何百万人の子供たちが見えるようになりたいと思った
like Crockett, /	クロケットのよう（な姿）に,
so they bought /	だから買った
these hats. //	これらの帽子を。

⇒別冊 p.34 ~ 35

Davy Crockett

Davy Crockett was born in the United States in 1786. His parents had nine children, so it was hard to get food for everyone. He learned how to shoot a gun when he was just eight years old so he could kill animals for food. When he was 12, he helped to take cows on a 600-kilometer trip. When Crockett was 14, his father wanted him to go to school. Crockett did not like it, so he left home.

Crockett loved to be in the forest, and he knew a lot about animals. A long time ago, many people ate bear meat. Also, people did not have electricity, so they made candles from bear fat. Bears were dangerous animals, but it was important to hunt them for food and safety. In one year, Crockett killed 105 of these animals. That made him very famous.

Later, Crockett went to Texas. Today, Texas is a state in America. But in those days, Texas was part of Mexico. People in Texas did not like Mexico. They wanted Texas to be free. Crockett went and fought with them. He was in a battle at a church called the Alamo in 1836. He died, but the battle became famous because the people were fighting to be free.

In the 1950s, a TV show was made about Crockett. The show became one of the world's most famous TV shows. In the show, Crockett wore a special hat called a "coonskin cap." It was made of raccoon fur. Millions of children wanted to look like Crockett, so they bought these hats.

デイビー・クロケット

デイビー・クロケットは1786年にアメリカ合衆国で生まれた。両親には子供が9人いたので，全員分の食べ物を手に入れるのは難しかった。彼はわずか8歳のときに，食料のために動物を殺すことができるように銃の撃ち方を学んだ。12歳のときには，ウシを600キロ移動させるのを手伝った。クロケットが14歳のとき，父は彼に学校に行ってほしかった。クロケットは学校が好きではなかったので，家出した。

クロケットは森の中にいるのが大好きで，動物についてたくさん知っていた。昔，多くの人はクマの肉を食べた。また，人々は電気を持っていなかったのでクマの脂肪からロウソクを作っていた。クマは危険な動物だったが，食料と安全のためにクマを狩ることは重要だった。1年で，クロケットはこれらの動物を105頭殺した。それは彼を非常に有名にした。

その後，クロケットはテキサスへ行った。今日ではテキサスはアメリカの州である。しかし当時，テキサスはメキシコの一部だった。テキサスの人々はメキシコが好きではなかった。彼らはテキサスが自由であることを望んだ。クロケットは行って彼らと一緒に戦った。1836年にアラモという名の教会で，彼は戦いに参加した。彼は死んだが，人々が自由になるために戦っていたのでその戦いは有名になった。

1950年代に，クロケットに関するテレビ番組が制作された。その番組は，世界で最も有名なテレビ番組の1つになった。番組の中で，クロケットは「クーンスキンキャップ」と呼ばれる特別な帽子をかぶっていた。それはアライグマの毛皮で作られていた。何百万人の子供たちが，クロケットのような姿になりたいと思って，この帽子を買った。

⇒別冊 p.36 ~ 37

解答と解説

解答

(1) ②　(2) ②　(3) ④　(4) ①　(5) ④

解説

(1) 第 1 段落の最後の 2 文の内容から考えて，**2** が正解。

設問・選択肢の和訳

(1) 2 月にデスバレーでは，…
× 1 通常摂氏(せっし) 40 度以上である。
○ 2 花を見ることができる。
× 3 1 年で最も暑い時期である。
× 4 毎日雨が降る。

(2) 第 2 段落の最後の 3 文の内容から考えて，**2** が正解。

設問・選択肢の和訳

(2) メスキートの木は…
× 1 900 年以上生きることができる。
○ 2 地下から水を得ることができる。
× 3 世界最大の葉を持つ。
× 4 毎日 5 センチ生長する。

(3) 第 3 段落の第 4・5 文の内容から考えて，**4** が正解。

設問・選択肢の和訳

(3) カンガルーネズミはいつ水を飲むか。
× 1 1 か月に 1 回。
× 2 1 日に 2 回。
× 3 夜だけ。
○ 4 ほとんど (飲ま) ない。

(4) 第 4 段落第 5 文の後半から第 6 文にかけて they called it “Death Valley.” But the Timbisha Shoshone do not like that name. とあるので，**1** が正解。

設問・選択肢の和訳

(4) ティンビシャ・ショショーニ族は…
○ 1 デスバレーという名前が好きではない。
× 2 デスバレーは暑くて怖いと思っている。
× 3 開拓者たちが水を見つけるのを手助けした。
× 4 デスバレーを出たがっている。

(5) 植物の説明は第２段落のみ，動物の説明は第３段落のみだから，１～３は不適切。**4** が正解。

設問・選択肢の和訳

(5) この話は…についてのものである
× 1 ある危険な植物。
× 2 植物が水を必要とする理由。
× 3 アメリカの動物。
○ 4 世界で最も暑い場所。

語句

DOWN LOAD

〈タイトル〉

- □ death (名) 死
- □ valley (名) 谷

〈第１段落〉

- □ desert (名) 砂漠
- □ almost (副) ほとんど

〈第２段落〉

- □ plant (名) 植物，草木

〈第３段落〉

- □ without (前) ～なしに
- □ all day 一日中
- □ come out 出てくる
- □ sometimes (副) 時には，時々
- □ not ～ at all まったく～ない
- □ air (名) 空気

〈第４段落〉

- □ thousand (名) 千
- □ scary (形) 怖い
- □ anywhere else 他のどこにも，他のどこでも

〈設問・選択肢〉

- □ leaves < leaf (名) 葉
- □ twice (副) ２度，２回

構造確認 ※誤読した部分の確認に使用してください。

⇒別冊 p.36 ~ 37

第1段落 アメリカのデスバレーは世界で最も暑い場所の１つだが，２月は訪れるにはよい時期である。

① Death Valley is a desert 〈in America〉.
S V C

デスバレーは〈アメリカにある〉砂漠である。

② It is the hottest place (on Earth).
S V C

そこは（地球上で）最も暑い場所である。

③ (In July) (in Death Valley), it is over 40℃ (almost every day).
S V C

（7 月には）（デスバレーでは），（ほぼ毎日）摂氏 40 度を超える。

④ Death Valley (also) had the hottest day (in the history 〈of the world〉) (on July 10, 1913).
S V O

デスバレーでは（また）（1913 年，7 月 10 日に）（〈世界の〉歴史上）最も暑い日になった。

⑤ It was 56℃.
S V C

摂氏 56 度だった。

⑥ People say [the best time 〈to visit〉 is (in February)].
S V O S' V'

[〈訪れるのに〉最もよい時期は（2 月に）ある] と人々は言う。

⑦ It is not so hot, and there are many flowers (then).
S① V① C① V② S②

（その時期には）それほど暑くなく，多くの花が咲いている。

第２段落 メスキートという木は非常に長い根を持ち，雨の少ないデスバレーでも水を引き上げられる。

① There are more than 900 kinds of plants (in Death Valley).

V　S

(デスバレーには) 900 を超える種類の植物がある。

② One is a very small tree 〈called mesquite〉.

S　V　C

1 つは〈メスキートと呼ばれる〉非常に小さな木である。

③ Death Valley (usually) gets (only) about 5 cm of rain (in a year).

S　V　O

デスバレーでは (通常) (1 年に) 約 5 センチの雨 (しか) (降ら) ない。

④ But mesquite has very long roots.

S　V　O

しかしメスキートは非常に長い根を持っている。

⑤ They can go down (more than 15 meters (into the ground)).

S　V

それらは ((地中) 15 メートルを超えて) のびることができる。

⑥ They bring water (up to the plant).

S　V　O

それらは水を (その植物まで) 引き上げる。

第３段落 水なしで長く生きられるオオツノヒツジや空気から水を得るカンガルーネズミなどがいる。

① There are (also) many animals.

V　S

多くの動物 (も) いる。

② Bighorn sheep can live (without water) (for over a month).

S　V

オオツノヒツジは (1 か月を超える期間を) (水なしで) 生きることができる。

③ Kangaroo rats sleep (all day) and (only) come (out at night).
S V① V②

カンガルーネズミは（昼間はずっと）眠り，（夜に外へ）出る（だけ）である。

④ And kangaroo rats (sometimes) do not drink water (at all). 

S V O

カンガルーネズミたちは（時には）（まったく）水を飲まないこともある。

⑤ Kangaroo rats get most 〈of the water 〈they need〉〉 (from the air and from [eating seeds and plants]). 注5
S V O S' V'

カンガルーネズミたちは〈〈必要とする〉水の〉大部分を（空気中から，そして［種や植物を食べること］から）得ている。

第４段落 ティンビシャ・ショショーニ族にとってデスバレーは故郷であり他のどこにも住みたくない。

① People 〈called the Timbisha Shoshone〉 have lived (in Death Valley) (for over a thousand years). 注6
S V

〈ティンビシャ・ショショーニ族と呼ばれる〉人々は（千年を超える間）（デスバレーに）住み続けている。

② (In the 1800s), some American pioneers went (there).
S V

（1800年代に），何人かのアメリカ開拓者たちが（そこに）行った。

③ They thought [Death Valley was hot and scary].
S V O S' V' C'

彼らは［デスバレーは暑くて怖いところだ］と思った。

④ The Timbisha Shoshone knew [how to find water], but the pioneers did not.
S① V① O① S② V②

ティンビシャ・ショショーニ族は［水の見つけ方］を知っていたが，開拓者たちは知らなかった。

⑤ Some 〈of the pioneers〉 died, so they called it "Death Valley".
S① V① S② V② O② C②

〈開拓者たちの〉何人かが死んだので，彼らはそこを「デスバレー（死の谷）」と呼んだ。

⑥ But the Timbisha Shoshone do not like that name.
S V O

しかしティンビシャ・ショショーニ族はその名前が好きではない。

⑦ Death Valley is their home, and they don't want to live (anywhere else).
S① V① C① S② V②

デスバレーは彼らの故郷であり，(他のどこにも) 住みたくないのだ。

注1 温度や天気，明暗を表す場合には，it という主語を使います。この it には「それ」という意味はありません。

注2 one は代名詞的に使われています。この場合は a plant という名詞の代わりに使われています。

注3 この文での for という前置詞は「～の間」という意味で期間を表しています。over は「～を超えて」という意味なので，for over a month で「1ヶ月を超える期間」という意味になります。

注4 not ... at all は「まったく…ない」という意味で，完全に否定してしまう場合に使われる表現です。

注5 they need の部分が，直前の名詞 water を修飾しています。water の直後に，that や which という関係代名詞が省略されていると考えることもできます。

注6 have[has] ＋過去分詞 は現在完了形です。この現在完了形は過去から続いている物事の現状を表しています。この文では，この部族が過去から現在まで継続的にこの地域に住んでいることを表しています。

Unit 19

サイトトランスレーション

⇒別冊 p.36 ~ 37

1 Death Valley is a desert /	デスバレーは砂漠である
in America. //	アメリカにある。
It is the hottest place /	それは最も暑い場所である
on Earth. //	地球で。
In July /	7月には
in Death Valley, /	デスバレーでは,
it is over 40°C /	摂氏40度を超える
almost every day. //	ほぼ毎日。
Death Valley also had /	またデスバレーにはあった
the hottest day /	最も暑い日が
in the history /	歴史上
of the world /	世界の
on July 10, 1913. //	1913年の7月10日に。
It was 56°C. //	摂氏56度だった。
People say /	人々は言う
the best time /	最もよい時期は
to visit /	訪れるのに
is in February. //	2月にあると。
It is not so hot, /	それほど暑くなく,
and there are many flowers then. //	その時期には多くの花が咲く。
2 There are more than 900 kinds /	900を超える種類がある

of plants /	植物の
in Death Valley. //	デスバレーには。
One is a very small tree /	1 つは非常に小さな木である
called mesquite. //	メスキートと呼ばれる。
Death Valley usually gets /	通常デスバレーでは得る
only about 5 cm /	ほんの約 5 センチメートルだけの
of rain /	雨を
in a year. //	1 年に。
But mesquite has /	しかしメスキートは持っている
very long roots. //	非常に長い根を。
They can go down /	それらはのびることができる
more than 15 meters /	15 メートルを超えて
into the ground. //	地中に。
They bring /	それらは引き上げる
water /	水を
up to the plant. //	その植物まで。
3 There are also many animals. //	多くの動物もいる。
Bighorn sheep can live /	オオツノヒツジは生きることができる
without water /	水なしで
for over a month. //	1 か月を超える期間を。
Kangaroo rats sleep /	カンガルーネズミは眠る
all day /	昼間はずっと
and only come out /	そして外へ出るだけだ
at night. //	夜に。

And kangaroo rats /	カンガルーネズミたちは
sometimes do not drink /	時には飲まないこともある
water /	水を
at all. //	まったく。
Kangaroo rats get /	カンガルーネズミたちは得る
most of the water /	水の大部分を
they need /	彼らが必要とする
from the air /	空気から
and from eating seeds and plants. //	そして種や植物を食べることから。
4 People /	人々は
called the Timbisha Shoshone /	ティンビシャ・ショショーニ族と呼ばれる
have lived /	住んでいる
in Death Valley /	デスバレーに
for over a thousand years. //	千年を超える間。
In the 1800s, /	1800 年代に,
some American pioneers went /	何人かのアメリカ開拓者たちが行った
there. //	そこに。
They thought /	彼らは思った
Death Valley was hot and scary. //	デスバレーは暑くて怖いところだと。
The Timbisha Shoshone knew /	ティンビシャ・ショショーニ族は知っていた
how to find /	見つけ方を
water, /	水の,
but the pioneers did not. //	しかし開拓者たちは知らなかった。
Some of the pioneers died, /	開拓者たちの何人かは死んだ,

so they called /	そのため彼らは呼んだ
it /	そこを
“Death Valley.” //	「デスバレー（死の谷）」と。
But the Timbisha Shoshone do not like /	しかしティンビシャ・ショショーニ族は好きではない
that name. //	その名前が。
Death Valley is their home, /	デスバレーは彼らの故郷であり，
and they don’t want to live /	彼らは住みたくない
anywhere else. //	他のどこにも。

問題英文と全訳

⇒別冊 p.36 ~ 37

Death Valley

Death Valley is a desert in America. It is the hottest place on Earth. In July in Death Valley, it is over 40°C almost every day. Death Valley also had the hottest day in the history of the world on July 10, 1913. It was 56°C. People say the best time to visit is in February. It is not so hot, and there are many flowers then.

There are more than 900 kinds of plants in Death Valley. One is a very small tree called mesquite. Death Valley usually gets only about 5 cm of rain in a year. But mesquite has very long roots. They can go down more than 15 meters into the ground. They bring water up to the plant.

There are also many animals. Bighorn sheep can live without water for over a month. Kangaroo rats sleep all day and only come out at night. And kangaroo rats sometimes do not drink water at all. Kangaroo rats get most of the water they need from the air and from eating seeds and plants.

People called the Timbisha Shoshone have lived in Death Valley for over a thousand years. In the 1800s, some American pioneers went there. They thought Death Valley was hot and scary. The Timbisha Shoshone knew how to find water, but the pioneers did not. Some of the pioneers died, so they called it "Death Valley." But the Timbisha Shoshone do not like that name. Death Valley is their home, and they don't want to live anywhere else.

デスバレー（死の谷）

デスバレーはアメリカにある砂漠である。そこは地球上で最も暑い場所である。デスバレーでは7月には，ほぼ毎日摂氏40度を超える。1913年7月10日には，デスバレーでは世界の歴史上最も暑い日にもなった。摂氏56度だった。訪れるのに最もよい時期は2月だと人々は言う。その時期にはそれほど暑くなく，多くの花が咲く。

デスバレーには900を超える種類の植物がある。1つはメスキートという名の非常に小さな木である。デスバレーでは通常，1年にわずか約5センチの雨しか降らない。しかしメスキートは非常に長い根を持っている。根は地中に15メートルを超えてのびることができる。根は水をその植物まで引き上げる。

多くの動物もいる。オオツノヒツジは1か月を超える期間を水なしで生きることができる。カンガルーネズミは昼間はずっと眠り，外へ出るのは夜だけである。カンガルーネズミたちは時にはまったく水を飲まないこともある。カンガルーネズミたちは必要とする水の大半を空気中から，そして種や植物を食べることから得ている。

ティンビシャ・ショショーニ族と呼ばれる人々は，千年を超える間デスバレーに住んでいる。1800年代に，アメリカ開拓者たちの一部がそこに行った。彼らはデスバレーが暑くて怖いところだと思った。ティンビシャ・ショショーニ族は水の見つけ方を知っていたが，開拓者たちは知らなかった。開拓者たちの何人かが死んだので，彼らはそこを「デスバレー（死の谷）」と呼んだ。しかし，ティンビシャ・ショショーニ族はその名前が好きではない。デスバレーは彼らの故郷であり，他のどこにも住みたくないのだ。

⇒別冊 p.38 ~ 39

解答と解説

解答

(1) ① (2) ④ (3) ③ (4) ① (5) ②

解説

(1) 第1段落第2文の後半から第3・4文にかけて she had a problem. She and her parents lived in a place, called Derbyshire in England. It is far from the ocean. とあるので，**1** が正解。

設問・選択肢の和訳

(1) エレン・マッカーサーの問題は何だったか。
○1 海から遠くに住んでいた。
×2 セーリングの本を手に入れることができなかった。
×3 おばの船が安全ではなかった。
×4 両親がセーリングを好きではなかった。

(2) 第2段落第3・4文の in 1995, when she was 17, she had enough money to get one. That same year, she sailed her new boat all around the country. から考えて，**4** が正解。

設問・選択肢の和訳

(2) マッカーサーが17歳のとき，彼女は…
×1 初めてセーリングに行った。
×2 お金を貯め始めた。
×3 セーリングに関する本を買った。
○4 イングランド中に自分の船を帆走(はんそう)させた。

(3) 第3段落第1・2・3文の内容から考えて，**3** が正解。

設問・選択肢の和訳

(3) マッカーサーが初めて世界一周の帆走をしたのはいつか。
×1 1980年。
×2 1995年。
○3 2001年。
×4 2005年。

(4) 第4段落第7・8文の内容から考えて，**1** が正解。

設問・選択肢の和訳

(4) 今日では，エレン・マッカーサーは…
○1 人々にリサイクルを教える団体を持っている。
×2 毎年セーリングのレースに参加する。

×3 帆走中に鳥を研究している。
×4 若者にセーリングについて教えている。

(5) 本文によればエレン・マッカーサーはセーリングの選手だったので，**2** が正解。

設問・選択肢の和訳

(5) この話は…についてのものである
×1 セーリングの話の作者。
○2 セーリングが上手なある女性。
×3 新しい種類の船を造ったある女性。
×4 海鳥を研究するある科学者。

語句

〈第1段落〉

□ take ～ sailing	～をセーリング［帆走］に連れて行く
□ far from ～	～から遠くに
□ ocean	(名) 海
□ dream about ～	～について夢見る
□ own	(形) 自分自身の

〈第2段落〉

□ save money	お金を貯める，貯金する
□ cheap	(形) 安い，安価な
□ clothes	(名) 服
□ finally	(副) ついに，とうとう
□ enough	(形) 十分な
□ sail	(動) (船を) (帆で) 走らせる，帆走する
□ same	(形) 同じ

〈第3段落〉

□ enter	(動) ～に参加する
□ race	(名) レース，競走
□ alone	(副) ひとりで
□ on *one*'s first try	初めての試行［挑戦］で
□ set a world record	世界記録を打ち立てる

〈第4段落〉

□ keep ～ing	～し続ける
□ race	(動) レース［競走］をする
□ one day	ある日
□ stop O from ～ing	O が～するのを止める，O に～するのをやめさせる
□ hurt	(動) ～を傷つける
□ recycle	(動) リサイクル［再生利用］する
□ sailor	(名) 帆走者，セーリングの選手，船乗り

〈設問・選択肢〉

□ safe	(形) 安全な
□ for the first time	初めて
□ seabird	(名) 海鳥

構造確認 ※誤読した部分の確認に使用してください。

⇒別冊 p.38 ~ 39

第 1 段落 エレン・マッカーサーは 4 歳でセーリングと出会い，自分の船を持つことを夢見始めた。

① (In 1980), (when Ellen MacArthur was four years old), her aunt took her sailing.
S' V' C' S V O

(1980 年に)，(エレン・マッカーサーが 4 歳のとき)，おばが彼女をセーリングをしに連れて行った。

② She loved it, and she wanted to do it (every day), but she had a problem.
S① V① O① S② V② O② S③ V③ O③

彼女はそれが大好きで (毎日) したかったが，1 つの問題があった。

③ She and her parents lived (in a place 〈called Derbyshire〉 〈in England〉).
S V

彼女と両親は (〈イングランドの〉〈ダービーシャーという〉場所に) 住んでいた。

④ It is far (from the ocean).
S V C

そこは (海から) 遠い。

⑤ She started [reading many books 〈about sailing〉] and dreamed (about [having her own boat]).
S V① O① V②

注1

彼女は [〈セーリングに関する〉多くの本を読み] 始め，([自分自身の船を持つこと] について) 夢見た。

第 2 段落 彼女は船を買うために 10 歳のとき貯金を始め，17 歳で自分の船を買って国中を帆走した。

① (When MacArthur was 10), she started [saving money].
S' V' C' S V O

(マッカーサーが 10 歳のとき)，彼女は [貯金] を始めた。

② She bought cheap clothes and cheap food (so she could get money 〈for a boat〉).

S① V① O① S② V② O②

（彼女は〈ボートのための〉お金を得られるよう）安い服と安い食べ物を買った。

③ (Finally), (in 1995), (when she was 17), she had enough money 〈to get one〉.

S' V' C' S V O

（ついに），（1995年に），（彼女が17歳だったとき），〈船を買うのに〉十分なお金が貯まった。

④ (That same year), she sailed her new boat (all around the country).

S V O

（その同じ年に），彼女は自分の新しい船を（国中）帆走させた。

第３段落 彼女は24歳で世界一周レースに初挑戦し人々を驚かせ，４年後に世界記録を打ち立てた。

① (In 2001), MacArthur entered the Vendée Globe.

S V O

（2001年に），マッカーサーはヴァンデ・グローブに参加した。

② It is a race 〈around the world〉.

S V C

それは〈世界一周〉レースである。

③ She did not win, but people were surprised that a young woman could sail (around the world) (alone) (on her first try).

S① V① S② V② C② S' V'

注4

彼女は勝たなかったが，人々は若い女性が（初挑戦で）（一人で）（世界中を）帆走できたことに驚いた。

④ She was (only) 24.

S V C

彼女は（たった）24歳だった。

⑤ (In 2005), she sailed (around the world) (again).

S V

（2005年に），彼女は（再び）（世界中を）帆走した。

⑥ (This time), she set a world record.
S V O

(今回は)，彼女は世界記録を打ち立てた。

⑦ She made the trip (in (just) 71 days).
S V O

彼女は((わずか) 71 日で) 帆走を成しとげた。

第 4 段落 彼女は優れた船乗りだったが今はレースをやめ，地球をよりよい場所にするため働いている。

① MacArthur became very famous.
S V C

マッカーサーはとても有名になった。

② She was young, and people thought [she would keep racing].
S① V① C① S② V② O②S' V' O'

彼女は若く，人々は [彼女がレースを続けるだろう] と思っていた。

③ But she wanted to do something different.
S V O

しかし彼女は何か違うことがしたかった。

④ (One day), (while she was sailing), she saw birds being killed.
S' V' S V O C

(ある日)，(彼女はセーリング中に)，鳥が殺されているのを見た。

⑤ She wanted to stop people (from [hurting nature]).
S V O

彼女は人々に ([自然を傷つけるの] を) やめさせたいと思った。

⑥ She stopped racing.
S V O

彼女はレースをやめた。

⑦ She started a group 〈called the Ellen MacArthur Foundation〉 (in 2009).
S V O

(2009年に) 彼女は〈エレン・マッカーサー財団という〉団体を始めた。

⑧ It teaches people to recycle.
S V O

その団体は人々にリサイクルするようにと教える。

⑨ She was a great racer and a great sailor, but (now) she is working (hard) (to make Earth a better place).
S① V① C① S② V②

彼女は優れたレーサーであり優れた船乗りだったが，(今では) (地球をよりよい場所にするために) (一生けんめい) 働いている。

注1 動詞の～ing形にはさまざまな使い方がありますが，その一つが「動名詞」です。「～すること」という意味で動詞に名詞の働きをさせ，動詞や前置詞の目的語にすることができます。

注2 so (that) S can Vは「SがVできるように」という意味で，何かをする目的を表すことができます。ここでは，時制の統一のためにcanの過去形couldが使われています。

注3 all around ～は「～中(じゅう)を」という意味の前置詞の働きをする表現です。

注4 be surprised that S Vは「SがVして驚く」という意味の表現です。that以下は驚いた理由を表しています。

注5 stop O from ～ingは「Oが～するのを止める，Oに～するのをやめさせる」という意味の表現です。

注6 make O Cは「OをCにする」という意味で用いられています。

Unit 20

サイトトランスレーション

⇒別冊 p.38 ~ 39

1 In 1980, /	1980 年に,
when Ellen MacArthur was four years old, /	エレン・マッカーサーが 4 歳のとき,
her aunt took /	おばが連れて行った
her /	彼女を
sailing. //	セーリングしに。
She loved it, /	彼女はそれが大好きだった,
and she wanted to do it /	そしてそれをしたかった
every day, /	毎日,
but she had /	しかし彼女は持っていた
a problem. //	1 つの問題を。
She and her parents lived /	彼女と両親は住んでいた
in a place /	場所に
called Derbyshire /	ダービーシャーという
in England. //	イングランドの。
It is far /	そこは遠い
from the ocean. //	海から。
She started /	彼女は始めた
reading many books /	多くの本を読むことを
about sailing /	セーリングに関する
and dreamed /	そして夢見た
about having /	持つことを

her own boat. //	自分自身の船を。
2 When MacArthur was 10, /	マッカーサーが 10 歳のとき,
she started /	彼女は始めた
saving money. //	貯金を。
She bought /	彼女は買った
cheap clothes and cheap food /	安い服と安い食べ物を
so she could get /	手に入れられるよう
money /	お金を
for a boat. //	ボートのための。
Finally, /	ついに,
in 1995, /	1995 年に,
when she was 17, /	彼女が 17 歳のとき,
she had enough money /	十分なお金が貯まった
to get one. //	船を買うのに。
That same year, /	その同じ年に,
she sailed /	彼女は帆走させた
her new boat /	自分の新しい船を
all around the country. //	国中に。
3 In 2001, /	2001 年に,
MacArthur entered /	マッカーサーは参加した
the Vendée Globe. //	ヴァンデ・グローブに。
It is a race /	それはレースである
around the world. //	世界一周の。
She did not win, /	彼女は勝たなかった,

but people were surprised /	しかし人々は驚いた
that a young woman could sail /	若い女性が帆走できたことに
around the world /	世界中を
alone /	1人で
on her first try. //	初挑戦で。
She was only 24. //	彼女はたった24歳だった。
In 2005, /	2005年に,
she sailed /	彼女は帆走した
around the world /	世界中を
again. //	再び。
This time, /	今回は,
she set /	彼女は打ち立てた
a world record. //	世界記録を。
She made /	彼女は成しとげた
the trip /	帆走を
in just 71 days. //	わずか71日で。
4 MacArthur became /	マッカーサーはなった
very famous. //	とても有名に。
She was young, /	彼女は若かった,
and people thought /	そして人々は思った
she would keep /	彼女は続けるだろうと
racing. //	レースを。
But she wanted to do /	しかし彼女はしたかった
something different. //	何か違うことを。

One day, /	ある日,
while she was sailing, /	彼女はセーリング中に,
she saw /	見た
birds /	鳥を
being killed. //	殺されている。
She wanted to stop /	彼女はやめさせたかった
people /	人間に
from hurting nature. //	自然を傷つけることを。
She stopped /	彼女はやめた
racing. //	レースを。
She started /	彼女は始めた
a group /	団体を
called the Ellen MacArthur Foundation /	エレン・マッカーサー財団という
in 2009. //	2009 年に。
It teaches /	その団体は教える
people /	人々に
to recycle. //	リサイクルするようにと。
She was a great racer /	彼女は優れたレーサーだった
and a great sailor, /	そして優れた船乗りだった,
but now /	しかし今では
she is working /	彼女は働いている
hard /	一生けんめい
to make Earth a better place. //	地球をよりよい場所にするために。

⇒別冊 p.38 ~ 39

Ellen MacArthur

In 1980, when Ellen MacArthur was four years old, her aunt took her sailing. She loved it, and she wanted to do it every day, but she had a problem. She and her parents lived in a place called Derbyshire in England. It is far from the ocean. She started reading many books about sailing and dreamed about having her own boat.

When MacArthur was 10, she started saving money. She bought cheap clothes and cheap food so she could get money for a boat. Finally, in 1995, when she was 17, she had enough money to get one. That same year, she sailed her new boat all around the country.

In 2001, MacArthur entered the Vendée Globe. It is a race around the world. She did not win, but people were surprised that a young woman could sail around the world alone on her first try. She was only 24. In 2005, she sailed around the world again. This time, she set a world record. She made the trip in just 71 days.

MacArthur became very famous. She was young, and people thought she would keep racing. But she wanted to do something different. One day, while she was sailing, she saw birds being killed. She wanted to stop people from hurting nature. She stopped racing. She started a group called the Ellen MacArthur Foundation in 2009. It teaches people to recycle. She was a great racer and a great sailor, but now she is working hard to make Earth a better place.

エレン・マッカーサー

1980年に，エレン・マッカーサーが4歳のとき，おばが彼女をセーリングに連れて行った。彼女はそれが大好きで毎日したかったが，1つの問題があった。彼女と両親は，イングランドのダービーシャーという場所に住んでいた。そこは海から遠い。彼女はセーリングに関する多くの本を読み始め，自分の船を持つことを夢見た。

マッカーサーは10歳のとき，貯金を始めた。ボートを買うお金を得られるよう，彼女は安い服と安い食べ物を買った。17歳になった1995年に，ついに船を買えるだけのお金が貯まった。その同じ年に，彼女は自分の新しい船で国中を帆走した。

2001年に，マッカーサーはヴァンデ・グローブに参加した。それは世界一周レースである。彼女は勝たなかったが，若い女性が初挑戦ながら1人で世界中を帆走できたことに人々は驚いた。彼女はまだ24歳だった。2005年に，彼女は再び世界中を帆走した。このときは，彼女は世界記録を打ち立てた。彼女はわずか71日で帆走を成しとげた。

マッカーサーはとても有名になった。彼女は若く，レースを続けるだろうと人々は思っていた。しかし，彼女は何か違うことがしたかった。ある日，セーリング中に，彼女は鳥が殺されているのを見た。彼女は人間が自然を傷つけることをやめさせたかった。彼女はレースをやめた。2009年に，彼女はエレン・マッカーサー財団という団体を始めた。その団体は人々にリサイクルを教える。彼女は優れたレーサーであり，優れた船乗りだったが，今では地球をよりよい場所にするために一生けんめい働いている。

●英文校閲　Karl Matsumoto

英語4技能　ハイパートレーニング
長文読解（2）基礎編

2020年2月1日　初　版第1刷発行

監修者	安河内 哲也 アンドリュー・ロビンス
発行人	門間 正哉
発行所	株式会社 桐原書店 〒160-0023 東京都新宿区西新宿4-15-3 住友不動産西新宿ビル3号館 TEL：03-5302-7010（販売） www.kirihara.co.jp
装丁・本文レイアウト	戸塚 みゆき（ISSHIKI）
DTP	有限会社マーリンクレイン
印刷・製本	図書印刷株式会社

ISBN978-4-342-20581-1
Printed in Japan